SUCCESS WITH SALMON

SUCCESS WITH
SALMON

Crawford Little

DAVID & CHARLES
Newton Abbot London North Pomfret (Vt)

Photographs by Arthur Oglesby, Eric Chalker and J. C. Little
Line illustrations by the author

British Library Cataloguing in Publication Data

Little, Crawford
   Success with salmon.
   1. Salmon-fishing
   I. Title
   799.1'755   SH684

ISBN 0-7153-9102-X

Typeset by Typesetters (Birmingham) Ltd
Smethwick West Midlands
and printed in Great Britain
by Butler & Tanner Limited Frome and London
for David & Charles Publishers plc
Brunel House   Newton Abbot   Devon

Published in the United States of America
by David & Charles Inc
North Pomfret   Vermont 05053   USA

CONTENTS

To Carolyn

*Friend, partner, wife, mother of our children
and far too good for the likes of me*

INTRODUCTION

I caught my first fish in the last autumn of total freedom before starting school. It was a roach, a tiny fish caught on float and worm. But it was the start of a hobby, a sport, a dedication and eventually an obsession that was to effect the whole course of my life.

For three years, my father waited patiently. I would stare at the gaily coloured float for hours, while he gazed at the sailing dinghies that tacked and reached along the reservoir's distant, concrete shore. Then he could stand it no longer. He had fished throughout his boyhood and youth in the Scottish Borders, but the fish he knew were the wild, brown trout. Something had to be done to get me away from that damned float.

The following spring, we travelled north to Speyside for my seventh birthday. Captain Tommy Edwards ran game-fishing courses from the Palace Hotel in Grantown. Tommy had something of a reputation. He did not suffer fools gladly. Even at my tender age, I could tell that there were some fools on that course. The Captain would become gruff and distant when he had been dealing with them.

My father quickly realised that the way with Tommy was to put yourself entirely in his hands. On the first morning, the Captain marched us into Mortimer's shop. Some time later, we emerged from this Aladdin's Cave, both carrying a Hardy split-cane fly rod and reel, the then new, plastic Aircel lines, waders and landing nets. Tommy chose the tackle, and he chose it well.

That was my first lesson in game fishing. You must get the foundations right, and that means balanced tackle suitable for your needs. As in most things, you tend to get what you pay for.

We also bought spools of fine nylon for leaders, although we still called them casts in those days, and a selection of artificial wet flies to tempt trout feeding below the surface. I already knew that a dry fly floated on the surface but a wet fly sank. I was mesmerised by boxes full of hooks delicately adorned with fur, feather and tinsel, and entranced by the magical and evocative names given to the individual patterns.

The salmon flies particularly caught my eye. I stared at the Thunder and Lightning, Jock Scott, Silver Grey and Yellow Torrish. It would be years before I learnt that, while the choice of pattern can be important, it is the size and design of the fly and, above all, how it is fished, that makes the difference between failure and success with salmon.

As we were packing the tackle away from the shop counter, Father nearly gave the game away. He had brought along his old and much worn wicker creel to

carry the odds and ends. Tyros' tackle should all look shiny and new. Tommy turned on him: 'I thought you said you were new to this game.' Father simply smiled, and told Tommy that he had inherited it.

That afternoon, I had my next lesson in fishing. I was handed over to Jack Martin to be taught to cast. No matter how much you spend, if you don't know how to use your tackle to its full advantage, you are simply wasting money, time and effort.

Like Tommy, Jack is sadly no longer with us. I reintroduced myself to him a few years ago at the Game Fair where he thrilled the crowds with his displays of casting. He could flick a cigarette from a pretty girl's mouth at twenty paces. Jack remembered the youngest angler that they had on the courses but, as he said: 'Eeh, you've grown a bit since them days, lad.' I suppose I have.

Casting lessons and fishing took up the rest of the week. I watched the salmon fishermen and thought that just as soon as I was able to wield those long, double-handed rods, that would be the sport for me. I saw the king of fish leaping or showing in his lair and knew that the days of floats, worms, roach, dace and gudgeon were over.

The last day was to be a fun competition, with prizes for the biggest catch of fish. Well, the adults might have been pretending that it was just for fun, but one small boy was taking it very seriously.

My father made a few discreet enquiries, and then booked a boat on Lochindorb. We would give the river a miss. Father spent the whole day acting as my ghillie on the oars, easing the boat around little headlands, clothed in heather, and into rocky bays. For some childish notion, I decided to keep the cast of flies that I used that day. I still have them, for posterity I suppose: a Peter Ross on the point, Greenwell's Glory on the centre and a Black Pennel on the bob. They enjoy their long retirement in the flap pocket of a wallet, together with the fly on which I caught my first salmon. Sentimental, you may say, but they mean a lot to me.

When we packed up to be back at the hotel for the weighing-in ceremony, I had twenty-three brown trout. We reckoned that I was in with a good chance. The only dark cloud on my horizon was that somebody might have caught a salmon.

We arrived at the hotel, and the hall tables were filled with silver platters piled high with heaps of salmon. At least one of them looked to be close to 30lb. Nigel Grant saw my crestfallen look and came over. 'Don't worry Crawford, all those fish were caught by the Palmers' party on their private beat.' Guests on the course were all fishing the Association water.

I had won the competition. Captain Tommy beamed and ruffled my hair. 'Well done the boy, and you won't be needing this now,' he said producing a round cast box filled with cast carriers. He had bought it for me as a consolation prize. Instead, I got a set of table mats. I still feel that I missed out on that deal.

Every time a salmon is caught, our knowledge grows

However, it wasn't table mats or cast boxes that taught me a lesson that day. A dozen adults had fished for salmon and never moved a fin. Others had changed to their trout rods in the afternoon and caught a few fish. However, weight for weight, if the perseverance of just one of them had produced a salmon, that man would have won the prize.

The difference between trout and salmon fishing is like how you choose to eat a cake. In trout fishing, you slice the cake and eat each slice one at a time over a long period. In salmon fishing you must stare at the cake, feeling more and more hungry until that glorious moment arrives and you gobble it all down in one, sit back and feel utterly contented. But if you prefer to never feel particularly full, but there again never particularly empty, stick to trout fishing.

The family party that was fishing on the private beat taught me another lesson. If you have plenty of money and are prepared to spend it, you can go to the baker and buy lots of cakes! It may not always be so, but the surest short-cut to success with salmon in terms of fish on the bank lies with an open cheque book.

We were all invited to a ceilidh that night, a sort of farewell party. I learnt a few more lessons, such as some adults can drink whisky like children drink lemonade. I wasn't allowed to stay up late, but I was awake after the piper. He lurched back against the wall as he was playing. The fading drone of his pipes made a fair imitation of the death rattle of a cat as he slowly slid down the wall and into unconsciousness.

That was when my mother decided it was past time for small boys to be in their beds. But I couldn't get into it. The maids had presented me with an apple-pie bed, the sheets neatly turned back on themselves like an envelope. I was learning that, for adults at least, *après fish* can be as much fun as the actual fishing.

The next day, in brilliant sunshine, we set off back to Yorkshire. The twenty-three trout had spent the night in the hotel fridge. Because I was so proud of them, I wanted to take them home, to return like some conquering Caesar with his chain of prisoners and slaves.

The fish were in a plastic bag, ungutted, and the day was hot. Somewhere about Edinburgh, my father suggested opening the car windows. As we crossed the border at Carter Bar, people who had stopped to fill their lungs with good Scottish air were treated to the sight of a small boy clutching a bag of fish out of the back window of a fast moving car.

My mother's uncle lived near Durham and I felt that I must show him my fish. I think we were already retching as we swept into his drive. Uncle Jack was the perfect man to inspect my catch. He had fallen from a ladder some years previously, landing on his nose. He had no sense of smell. The rest of us retreated upwind as he dug the fish into his garden.

Father gently explained my next lesson: don't kill what you can't eat. It maybe wasn't so important in those fish-rich days, but now I wouldn't think of killing even half that number of trout in a day. And it is why I will not kill a gravid hen fish, coloured and heavy with spawn. We can argue that a dead fish is a dead fish and one less to spawn whether it is killed fresh or after it has been in the river for some time, but what on earth is the point of killing a fish that is hardly fit to eat when, if returned to the river with care, she can produce fresh fish for seasons to come?

We lived in Yorkshire for a few more years. Every summer weekend we would retreat from the city into the dales; great days of fine sport with trout. I added upstream clear water worming to my skills. Father now fished the dry fly more than the wet.

Whenever we were out in the car and came to a bridge, the self-same cry would come from the back seat, 'Dad, do you think there are any fish in there? Stop the car, Dad!'

We would look over the parapet and he would point out where trout lie on the edges of food lanes, corridors in the water where the current funnels insect larvae, emergent and spent flies. Sometimes, when they rested, the trout could be seen gently hovering on the edges of fast streams into which they could turn and accelerate downstream if threatened. I learnt a lot about trout from looking over bridges, and this was the foundation for learning to read a salmon river in later years.

If a fish was lying close into the bank, Father would tell me how he and his cousin Gavin Fleming could tickle any trout from the streams between Canonbie and Waterbeck. However, probably fearing 'Hospital Consultant on Poaching Charge' headlines, he left me to carry out my practical experiments in that particular art on my own.

I couldn't say whether it had anything to do with bridges and the stirring of boyhood memories but, just before I was into my teens, the family returned to Scotland. Dumfriesshire has been the family home for centuries, since the family arrived from Norway, via Normandy and Cheshire. William Wallace's sister married a Little, and her son, Edward, fought alongside his uncle in guerilla campaigns against the English. Eventually, the Wallace was captured and executed in the most foul and disgusting way. My family stuck around to settle old scores. The first opportunity came for the Scots at Bannockburn, the start of three hundred years of the bloodiest feuding, border raiding and guerilla fighting that the world has ever seen.

And now I was big enough to wield the double-handed weapon. Not a sword, you understand, but a double-handed salmon rod. Remember those days of plenty in the mid-sixties when our rivers were packed with salmon? I grabbed at the opportunity to learn fishing through experience. It was just as well that I did.

Ulcerative dermal necrosis was just around the corner. It filled our rivers with the stink of dead and dying fish. And the ocean feeding grounds of the salmon were discovered. The high seas around Greenland became a scene of massacre and mayhem.

At home, the market price of salmon soared. This encouraged the organisation of ruthless poaching gangs who blasted, poisoned and netted salmon in rivers. They had their counterparts at sea. Coastal poaching on the fringe of territorial waters, using mile upon mile of monofilament drift nets, became a massive problem. Forestry became the fashionable and commercially attractive alternative for upland ground. More recently, with the sad decline in grouse, forestry planting has accelerated still further. With its associated drainage schemes, it can destroy the salmon's spawning redds and change the very nature of the river. And there are many other problems such as industrial pollution, water impounding, abstraction and obstruction; the list goes on.

I was learning fast that the salmon resource is subject to heavy commercial and political pressure, and forced to compete with alternative land and water ventures. The salmon resource is far from infinite and must be protected, managed, nurtured and, whenever possible enhanced or it might collapse under the burdens so wantonly piled upon it.

The popular conservation movement was growing apace. We could look forward to the prospect of a better cared for environment and cleaner rivers, but there were two sides to the coin. The conservationists sought an end to seal culling, seals that eat salmon by the thousands of tons. Conservation moved on to total protection and preservation in the case of certain species of fish-eating birds that were no longer to be controlled.

By now I had left school. It might be more accurate to say that I wandered away from it. It was a navy cadet school, and so my intention was obviously to go into the services. However, I decided that first I should get some professional

Success for the modern, articulated fly armed with a treble hook

qualification against the day that I returned to civilian life. That is how I came to be studying accountancy in Edinburgh, with no intention of becoming an accountant.

I was playing rugby very seriously in those days. A loose ball in front of our posts; Gala forwards rushing onto it like a pack of terriers. Then five months in a neurosurgical ward while they put my head back on my shoulders. It gave me plenty of time to read and to think. To hell with what I had been planning and doing with my life. I wanted a job in the country with plenty of fishing and shooting.

I left Edinburgh to spend a year on the Earl of Annandale's estates, then studied rural estate management for three years at the Royal Agricultural College. After that I married the finest girl in the world and worked for the Duke of Buccleuch for a couple of years, and then the Duchy of Cornwall for a little longer. But I was fast learning that, the higher you climb the ladder the more you have to justify your existence. Life as a very junior trainee on Buccleuch's was one thing: we practically lived on venison, game and fish, there were more than twenty gamekeepers, stalkers, river watchers and ghillies, and I spent an inordinate amount of time with rod and gun. But now I spent little more time out of the office than anybody employed in a city. The dogs were getting fat and lazy. The writing was on the wall. Carolyn and I packed up our belongings and two small boys, returned to Scotland and started a publishing company. We launched *Countrysport*, a national magazine dealing with fishing, shooting and stalking.

Five years on, we have parted with the magazine in order to concentrate on writing and various other ventures. And that, my friend, is the long and torturous route to the writing of this book. I make no apology or excuse, only an explanation.

It may seem strange to have introduced this book on salmon fishing in terms of my own life. However, to write of fishing is to write of part of my life, and an important part. I do not live to fish, but a life without fishing, and salmon fishing in particular, could never be the same for me.

With that thought in mind, it is good for me to be able to say that the salmon, throughout it all, has shown itself to be a survivor. Indeed, on many rivers, they are already returning to something approaching their former glory.

Conservation interests and an environmentally conscious and aware society are providing us with cleaner rivers. Rivers which, not so long ago, resembled open sewers have been cleaned up and are now enjoying runs of salmon and sea trout. Government cannot drag its heels over acid rain for very much longer.

However, it will be up to all those involved in rod and line fishing for salmon to ensure that the river, estuaries, coasts and high seas are managed for the maximum benefit and productivity of salmon, and sport for ourselves. The will and depth of feeling is greater than ever before. It makes me confident that there is a great future for salmon fishing; a future for ourselves and for generations to come. And it gives me the confidence to write this book.

1
WHY A SALMON TAKES

The salmon is generally acknowledged to be a non-feeder in fresh water. Little wonder then that generations of fishermen have pondered the question why salmon ever take a fly, lure or bait. Experienced fishermen are able to predict general trends in salmon behaviour, whether or not there is a possibility of finding a taking fish, and the how, where, when and what of the most likely offering to achieve success. However, most of them feel that they are skating on very thin ice in making suggestions as to the 'why' of taking behaviour. Indeed there are many lucky souls who do not give the question any attention at all, and they are able to catch fish. Others, like myself, are blessed or cursed, depending upon your point of view, with the need to at least try to understand what is going on.

Some sort of understanding of the salmon's taking behaviour is fundamental to my own views on salmon fishing. The study has taught and suggested many possibilities; not least of which is that, while the fisherman who keeps his fly in the water for the maximum possible time is going to catch some fish, there are times when it is better to relax and conserve energy and concentration for those times when it pays to fish really long and very hard – a time to sow and a time to reap.

THEORY OF TAKING BEHAVIOUR

A simple creature   It is necessary to start from some basic point, and this is summed up very neatly in the book *Lake and Loch Fishing (for Salmon and Sea Trout)* by W. A. Adamson. He states: 'Fish cannot reason. Physiologically, they simply have not the brains. They merely react to environment and internal and external stimuli.'

From this simple truth, it is possible to work toward a theory as to why the salmon does or does not take. The theory is borne out in practice, and it shows the absolute folly of those who have been guilty of gifting salmon, or any species of fish, with powers of deduction equal to that of humans. No fish can think like

Generations have asked why a salmon takes, but this young angler is just happy that sometimes they do

Grace Oglesby with a salmon from salt water. Impossible, some would say, but salmon do not always play by the rules

a human, any more than a human can think like a fish or swop land and skin for water and scales. Scientists call the improper gifting of human qualities to the species of lower intelligence 'anthropomorphism'. I am afraid that there will be quite a few such words in this chapter. Believe me, I have tried to avoid them, but there seem to be very few equivalents in everyday language, or they lose something in the translation.

And so, having made my excuses, I can bring in the word 'mechano-morphism', which is something else that fishermen must guard against in considering salmon behaviour. It means that, just because they are simple creatures, we cannot treat salmon as machines, all responding to some pre-programmed behaviour pattern. They may be simple, but they are all individuals with their own little quirks and mannerisms. The environmental and external stimuli may be broadly similar for all the salmon in a given pool, but the internal stimuli of each individual fish have to be taken into account, as well as a number of other factors considered in this chapter.

Cause and effect   As non-scientific students of animal behaviour, we need only concern ourselves with the immediate causes of given effects in order that we may catch more fish. Although explanation can be at a highly sophisticated level, we need only sufficient for us to predict and understand the relation between cause and effect (stimulus and response) in regard to environmental conditions and the mood of the fish (antecedent conditions and motivational state).

The fisherman, in presenting his fly to a fish, is attempting to provide a stimulus to trigger off a desired response – the salmon takes the fly. As simple and as complicated as that. Incidentally, 'fly' throughout this chapter is a shorthand term to include all lures, spinners and baits.

Factors in response   There has been a tendency to offer a list of possible explanations as to why a salmon will take hold of a fly. Each possibility is then considered, to be rejected for various reasons according to fashion or the writer's taste, until only one possibility is left. The suggestions offered include aggression, boredom, fear, and going through the motions of feeding. One writer went so far as to draw a comparison with the chewing of gum! But surely, it must be wrong to consider this matter in terms of black and white, either or? There are many shades of grey and a host of factors involved in determining whether or not an individual fish will take.

Professor Hinde of Cambridge University Department of Zoology, writing in general terms about animal behaviour in his book *Ethology* (Fontana, 1982) has the following to say: 'Of course, any particular item of behaviour may be influenced by many external stimuli and by diverse and unrelated aspects of the individual's motivational state.' In other words, although we consider the fly and the fish's response to that alone, the salmon is responding to a number of stimuli: fear of surroundings, absence of appetite, memory of feeding, air and water temperature, the comfort of its temporary residence, barometric pressure, its sex drive. A cock fish may respond aggressively to any intruder on the spawning redds; the fish may be irritated by an injury; the possibilities and permutations are endless. In presenting our fly to the salmon, we must realise that the individual's response varies due to both internal and external stimuli of a very complex nature and to how these effect the salmon's motivational state and the level, if present at all, of its readiness to 'have a go'.

In a pool full of fish, only one or two may be stimulated into the desired response. Although the external stimuli, certainly the majority of them, can be readily gauged by the fisherman on the river bank, there are still things that are hard to understand. For example, at the start of the season, how does a salmon lying at the bottom of 10ft of water realise and respond to the fact that the air temperature has fallen below that of the water? Probably, in this instance, it is sufficient simply to know that it does, rather than dwell on possible explanations. The real mystery lies with the whole range of internal stimuli which effect the individual's motivational state, and these are extremely difficult to predict. However, that is not to say that it is impossible to make reasonable suggestions based on our experience of when salmon are fairly easy, difficult or damn near impossible to tempt.

Motivational state is constantly changing, and these changes are both temporary and reversible. The salmon that ignores a fly the first time it is fished down a pool may take it solidly the next time it is presented. On hard-fished Association water it is not an uncommon source of amusement to see a fish taken, almost literally, 'out of the back pocket' of a preceding fisherman. Of course, the man who grassed the fish will put it down to slick handling and skill; others will call it luck; certainly it appears that something has occurred to change the salmon's motivational state. And this points to the fact that a great deal of success in salmon fishing must rest with being in the right place at the right time, and that this is as important in terms of square yards of water and minutes as it is in regard to the right river at the best time of the season.

Conflict behaviour and disinhibition   At any one time, stimuli cause more than one type of behaviour. Internal and external stimuli may be in conflict to one another and the resultant actions may go either way, the fish may take or it may not. The scientific terms are 'conflict behaviour' and 'disinhibition'.

It is early June as I write these words. My attention is drifting toward the first of the sea trout, but a summer spate will bring in salmon and grilse. The weather and water have warmed, and the fish will be lying in relatively fast water. From experience I would expect any taking fish to show the greatest interest in quite a small fly, fished close to the surface. But why does it take any fly at all?

The dominant behaviour of the fish is to ignore the fly. It has stopped feeding on its return to fresh water. Its purpose is to spawn and, until it does so, its main desire is for a comfortable lie, a safe place to tarry on its upstream migration to the spawning redds. Then, for no immediately apparent reason and in contradiction to its general trend of behaviour, it seizes a fly.

It might be thought that the stimulus of the fly alone has been enough to re-awaken the desire to feed. The previously suppressed activity has been stimulated to overcome, for however brief a time, the normal behaviour. Another possibility, and the one that I would argue for, is that the fly has been presented at a time when causal factors, the reasons for the salmon's lack of interest in taking a fly, have been lowered. Any chance that a fisherman has of catching the fish will be lost as the initial inhibition regains control.

THEORY INTO PRACTICE

The basis of my thinking on salmon fishing is, therefore, that although the dominant behaviour of the fish is to ignore the fisherman's offering, there are times when this pattern is suppressed, if only for an instant. This allows the resurrection of that type of behaviour that was once normal and dominant, ie, the desire to feed. Also, either positively or unwittingly, we may be strengthening some other behaviour, possibly curiosity or anger. As I have said, the combinations and permutations are endless.

Salmon will fall for a well presented fly when their inhibitions lose control

With a little thought, it is possible to predict those times when we should fish long and hard, and other periods when conditions suggest that it is safe to take things easy. In saying that, it is necessary to define 'long and hard'. By it I mean fishing with total concentration and effort, and for as long as it takes. I know one man who personifies this approach, and who shows total commitment to his salmon fishing. When he judges that fish are likely to be in the taking mood, he is up at dawn and gets in a few hours before breakfast. Then it's back to the river with a packed lunch. The evening meal is a more leisurely affair, but taken early in order that he may fish on into the last of the light, often a deadly taking time. Not until the last of the light has faded from the western sky will he return for a late supper, and then to bed. He tends to fish like that all the time for his fishing is limited to a couple of weeks holiday, he has paid a considerable sum for the beat, and he wants to take the most from every moment.

However, few of us would want to keep up with his pace. Some take a far more relaxed approach, waiting for the magical moment to arrive; that is how the majority of resident fishermen behave, and those who are able to take longer over their fishing holidays. Recently, I was talking to a very experienced salmon fisherman who told me that, in the six weeks that he had been on the Spey, he reckoned that only one of the days had offered really good fishing conditions. And yet I suspected that salmon were being steadily caught throughout that time; conditions don't have to be perfect for fish to be caught.

Another fisherman, tremendously keen and experienced, says, when greeted with the news that fish are not taking: 'Well then, let's see what we can do to make them take.' It is from him that I learnt the need to vary tactics, carry a few aces up my sleeve and to strongly avoid a stereotyped approach to salmon fishing. In difficult conditions he keeps fishing, but only trickling along at fairly low speed; when conditions look promising, it's into turbo-charge.

Fishing skill   It may seem I am suggesting that salmon fishing is nothing more than being in the right place at the right time. Of course, this is very important, but so is fishing skill. Remember those tones of grey in regard to a salmon's taking behaviour. At one end of the scale, there is the fish that it is practically impossible to tempt with anything. The dominant behaviour pattern, not to show any interest in a fly, is firmly in control. At the other end of the scale there is the fish that, for however short a time, is quite disinhibited and may be induced to take practically anything, however badly it is presented. The first class of fish, the non-taker, is the most common of all. The second class, the free-taker, is a rare fish indeed.

A salmon ready for landing. The right place at the right time, but fishing skill is equally important

Most fish are probably teetering on the brink, and may take if presented with a strong and proper stimulus. These, I am sure, represent the majority of salmon that are entered in the fishing log. The fisherman's task is to present just the right additional stimulus, in the shape of the fly, to add to the other stimuli that are creating conflict behaviour, to suppress the dominant, non-taking behaviour pattern, to tip the balance in favour of disinhibition, and thus achieve success. As I said earlier: as simple and as complicated as that.

Our stimulus, the fly If we were to adopt a completely fresh approach to salmon fishing, without any knowledge of what salmon were known to have been tempted by in the past, we would probably design a fly that, as closely as possible, represented some creature that salmon are known to prey upon at sea. However, experience shows that such a fly does not work as well as some patterns which, on immediate inspection, bear little if any similarity to any known natural food item. We have learnt that our fly need not be an exact replica, either in appearance or behaviour. We tend, like caricaturists, to exploit this fact by exaggerating those features upon which response seems to depend. This exaggeration can be seen in many points of fly design: tinsel bodies and ribbing, a slim profile, the long and active wing of a Collie Dog fly and so on. Jungle cock cheeks represent the eyes or gill covers of small fish. The art lies in knowing just how far to take this exaggeration. There is a point at which a fly can lose its identity to the fish, just as a caricature can lose its identity.

It can also be the exaggerated stimulus that is most likely to provoke a response from a salmon. For example, the fly could be roughly similar in size and profile to a small fish that the salmon has preyed upon at sea. The natural may be incapable of swimming at speeds in excess of 3mph and so, normally, we will do all in our power to fish the fly as slowly as possible. However, there are times when, by fishing the artificial at more than the apparently logical speed, we reinforce the stimulus and achieve a strong predatory response from the salmon.

Why is this so? Why doesn't an artificial that is as close a replica as possible of the natural, in appearance and behaviour, always prove the best stimulus? Why is this concept of caricature so important? Again, we can find the answers to these questions in the study of animal behaviour. Those who state, for example, that it is unreasonable to fish small flies at speeds greater than those of which the natural is capable are thinking like humans and not really trying to understand the mind of a fish, a simple creature lacking in powers of reason and deduction.

An example from a scientific study of a species with similar 'brain power' to a fish helps us greatly in understanding the concepts of caricature and exaggeration. To be brief, two scientists, Baerends and Krujit, carried out certain experiments on gulls in 1973. They found that when eggs are removed a little distance from the nest, the gulls retrieve them by rolling them along the ground. Hence these tests became known as the 'egg-rolling experiments'. It was when the scientists substituted or added dummy eggs of various sizes and colours, alongside the naturals, that interesting discoveries were made. The gulls showed a preference not only for dummy eggs larger than the natural, but also for those of a very bright-green hue. And these preferences summated. In other words, the gulls showed the strongest preference for a big, bright-green dummy egg.

Think about that. If you took a human baby away from its mother and placed it next to an oversized green doll, would you expect the distraught mother to rush to pick up the doll in preference to the baby? But the gull did. And experience shows that fish are every bit as capable of making similar decisions that appear totally irrational to the human mind. In case the point is lost, it is necessary to emphasise that the gulls appeared to *actively prefer* the dummy to the natural.

What experiments have been carried out to discover the preferences of a salmon? Well, they have been going on for generations. Every time a new fly is tried and found to work, we know a little more. Every time we catch a fish on an established pattern, we are confirming the findings of earlier research workers. There is a wealth of information on the subject, which will be considered in later chapters.

2

WHEN AND WHERE A SALMON TAKES

I had been invited to spend a few days on the Beauly and, on arrival, was surprised to learn that the total catch for the previous week had been only two fish. Another tremendously keen fisherman had been up for a few days to fish with my hosts and, with that trio on the river, I knew that conditions must be bad for them to be achieving so little success.

Having fished for a few hours on the first morning, I was passing time, sitting on a rock, and considering a change of fly. Some would say that the pattern is unimportant but, if nothing else, a change restores confidence, brings fresh hope, and makes me fish more purposefully. The sunlight danced on the body of a Bourrach. Streamy water, the surface boiling and swirling from the effect of a boulder-strewn river bed, plus the bright sunlight? The Bourrach from Speyside that I had tied on a long-shanked Wilson double looked just the thing and quite marvellous with its oval ribbed, silver tinsel body to catch the light, and the long yellow wing and blue hackle and tail. I tied it to the leader, but continued to sit on the rock.

I looked downstream to where my hostess was fishing on down the pool ahead of me. She has won the ladies' salmon fly casting event at the Game Fair, and was putting out an awesome length of line. It was good just to sit and watch. Just then, a fish showed slightly upstream of her. There was nothing new in that; it had shown many times in the last few hours and we were practically old friends. Many fish that had long since lost the sheen of the sea were showing regularly in the apparently pointless way of resident fish. But the manner of this individual fish had changed. There was something about that last jump. It had looked more purposeful, as if the fish were responding to the urge to forge on upstream. I was off my rock and into the river in quick time. The fish had showed well out across the stream and I was soon at maximum casting range. In order to cover it, I had to cast more squarely than normally, but I was reassured. I had been told that Beauly fish will often show a preference for a fly presented quite squarely. This one did, and soon I was able to hustle it into the waiting net.

Later in the day, as the light faded, I hooked and landed another fish, handlining the fly in deep water below a steep bank close to the head of a pool. It

Salmon running a Norwegian river. Running and taking behaviour are intimately linked

seemed an obvious place to try for a running fish in the dusk. There, I have said it. Running fish can be caught. In fact, I believe that the majority of fish we catch are runners.

RUNNING FISH

In the previous chapter, I looked at the question of taking behaviour. I said that the successful fly is one that is presented at a time when the causal factors for the salmon's lack of interest in a fly have been lowered, and that as the initial inhibition regains control, the chances of catching the fish dwindle away. It also appears that the causal factors required for a fish to run are so inextricably linked to those creating disinhibition in terms of whether it is likely to seize a fly that they can, in general terms, be considered one and the same thing.

We can all cite examples of fish taken in conditions that are anything but conducive to salmon running. But these are exceptions and do not negate the fact that the majority of salmon are taken either just as the river begins to rise and, later, as it begins to fall and clear, continuing through to that time when the river falls to normal summer levels. Fish are running, and any considerations in regard to water and air temperature, barometric pressure, the height of the sun, the number of turns of ribbing on the fly or whether Jupiter is in alignment with Mars and a black cat crossed our path on the way to the river, all go by the board.

It must be made quite clear what the term 'running' means. In the widest context, all salmon are running in that they have entered from the sea and are making for the spawning redds even though for many months they may remain in one pool. What we really mean when we refer to running fish is that they are proceeding upstream. We include those fish that may be doing nothing more than cruising to the head of the pool before returning to their lies. They are not responding to some piscean urge to go for an evening stroll; their actions reflect their desire to be moving on to the redds. They may not be moving far but, to all intents and purposes, they are running fish, and behave as such.

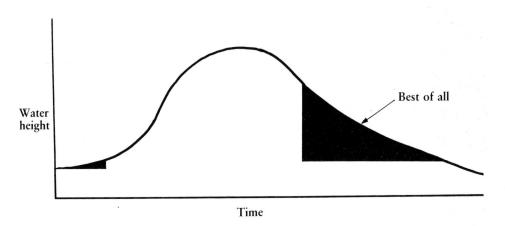

Taking times according to water height

Running on the water   Salmon run on a rise in river height. At the peak of the spate, the force of the current is such that they seek shelter in the quiet backwaters as if confident that, as the river begins to fall away and the current lessens, they will be able to forge on upstream. In fact, confidence doesn't come into it. They just realise that the push of the stream is too strong for them, and have no alternative but to wait for the stream to subside.

You will have seen a run of fish, hurrying on as if they knew that the time in which the river is at a fortuitous height is limited. Their sense of urgency as they shoulder their way through rapids and leap falls is a source of intense excitement for any sportsman and lover of nature. A single fish or a small group show in the tail of a pool; you chart their course by the purposeful, porpoise-like head and tail roll in the body of the pool. They may show again in the headstreams, and then they are off and away, continuing their migration.

I have said that the majority of fish that we catch are running, but what I really mean is that they are salmon which, in the general context of running, have

Water height, and our awareness of it, is vital to success with salmon

paused for a short rest. It is this pausing fish, this one catching its breath, that is most likely to seize a fly and which, above all others, is most likely to 'have a go'. However, when it is physically moving upstream it will ignore a fly, or any other offering that you may care to make, 99.9 per cent of the time.

It is as if the causal factors of the dominant behaviour – to run upstream and ignore any fly – become confused, and the greatest confusion seems to occur at those moments just as the fish is pausing and again just before he presses on. But any pausing fish is a likely taker.

The pausing fish Opinions differ, but it is generally estimated that a salmon, when actually moving upstream, may have a water speed of something approaching as much as 10mph. Certainly, I have seen a running fish enter a pool and, keeping it in sight, have practically had to trot to keep up with it as it swam through almost still water. Erring on the side of caution, let us use 7mph as the water speed of the fish. If it is swimming against a current of, say, an average of 3mph, its bank speed, its distance in regard to the river bed, will be about 4mph, the pace of a man walking quickly.

And so, if our beat is 40 miles upstream from the river mouth, and we know that a run of fish has come in on the tide and that running conditions are suitable, we might expect them to arrive in about 10 hours. We would be disappointed. Time and again, when we are able to measure the speed of running fish, we discover that they are only travelling a fraction of the distance we would expect. I was standing on Old Spey Bridge with Arthur Oglesby. He knows the Spey fishing well and, as we were discussing running fish, somebody asked him how long it took salmon to arrive at Grantown from Spey mouth. Arthur's reply indicated that the salmon appear to have a bank speed in the region of 1mph.

Some authorities have suggested even lower speeds. Richard Waddington in *Salmon Fishing: Philosophy and Practice* describes how he was fishing Crathie on the Dee at the end of April and how only one fish had been taken off the beat:

> One evening I heard from a friend who was fishing Monaltrie, immediately above Cambus o'May, that the fish had started, that afternoon, to move through the Glashan pool where he had taken a brace. The following day was a blank for me, but the day after I caught six fish on the Crathie water and the King's gillies caught a like number opposite me.

From this, he deduced that their average speed worked out at about 8 to 10 miles in 24 hours. He adds:

> This particular example is of a run of fish that was most anxious and determined to get up the river as they had been hanging about in the pools round Tassach and the Long Pool for a month or more. They travelled faster and with more determination, therefore, than the average run.

So, we have Arthur Oglesby suggesting a speed of 1mph on the Spey and Richard Waddington suggesting ⅓mph on the Dee. And this points very clearly, without citing any more authorities, that salmon, which are capable of moving upstream at about 4mph bank speed, must be pausing for about three-quarters

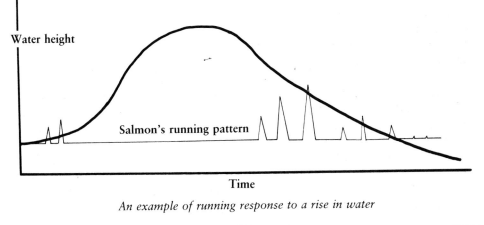

An example of running response to a rise in water

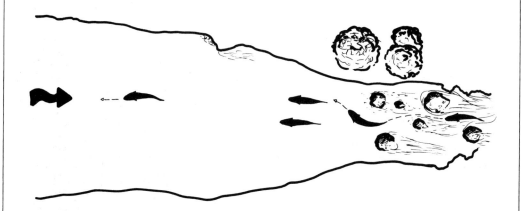

After facing a long stretch of broken water, salmon will pause in the tail of a pool before moving on

or more of the time that we say they are running. And it is during these pauses that they are most likely to be persuaded into taking a fly.

If I could choose conditions in which to fish, it would be in a high but clearing water following a good-sized spate; not enough to be worthy of the title 'flood' but certainly sufficient to get fish on the move. A favourite place to fish as the water is falling is the tail of a pool above a long stretch of broken water. A travelling fish that has fought its way up the rapids and white water will pause and rest, possibly only for the briefest of moments, and it is often a taking fish. Put a fly before it and bang! it is on. Fish persistently in the last yards of the pool, hanging the fly around rocks that bulge the surface.

During a drought, I was able to mark the position of a large slab of rock that had been worn into a saucer shape in the tail of a favourite pool. The knowledge was to swell my bag many times. It proved, as I expected, to be an attractive resting lie for a salmon before it made its way into the main pool; a place that I regard as a running lie, rather than a simpler and easily recognisable high-water lie. Similarly, it is possible to discover 'mini-pools' in an area of fast, streamy water. These may be large or, quite literally, the size of a table top. The thing to look for is an area of calm amid the maelstrom of broken water. If an inspection in times of low water reveals a flattish area, or a flat rock set amid the boulders, it should be marked down as a place where a running fish may choose to pause. Such spots cannot be described as wildly productive, and it has to be said that it can often be virtually impossible to fish a fly slowly across them without a hazardous wade but, when they save an otherwise blank day, they are more than worth knowing.

The tail of the pool may not be so good if the passage into the pool is an easy swim for the fish. In such a case, the salmon will not pause until it is right up in the neck, on the cheeks of the headstreams. This is another excellent place to try for a pausing fish.

Ghillies can predict when a run of fish will enter their beat

On spate rivers, fishing can come to a standstill if there is insufficient water

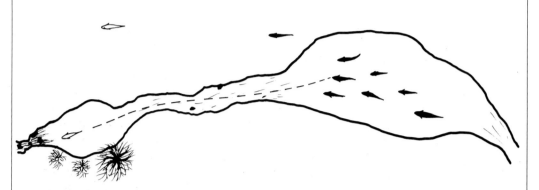

On a pool below the writer's house, fish move up from a large holding pool at dusk, and can be caught just below a stretch of rough, rapid water

Another good place is the first pool above a large holding pool. On the river below my house there is a great, deep dub of a pool known as the 'Long John'. Fish show in this pool all through the day at the back end of the season, when the Solway rivers are experiencing their main runs; but they are seldom caught. Upstream of this pool there is a series of streams which lead, eventually, into a small deep pool that carries a very heavy push of water in the neck. I like to be down there at dusk during a running water. Fish swim quickly out of the Long John, up through the streams and into the smaller pool. They pause as they reach the strong stream. One evening, I lit a cigarette, cast, and was into a fish. Before I had finished the cigarette, I was admiring the second of the brace – quite incredible sport. Two fishermen had been fishing the Long John all day with fly, worm and spinner. I couldn't claim to be any more skilful than they; the real reason why I was home with two fish after half an hour while they returned fishless was that I happened to be in the right place at the right time. There again, I wasn't there entirely by accident.

High-water running conditions seem to really bring out the predatory instinct in salmon. There is seldom anything tentative about the take, with fish often taking in a broad sweeping arc that sets the reel screaming from the word go! A long Collie Dog fly can be tremendously productive at such times.

HEIGHT OF WATER AND PROSPECTS

A graph of a river's height throughout a season would show a pattern of fast rises following heavy rain or a large snow melt, and more gentle falls as the increased water supply falls away. Near ideal conditions exist where the peaks and troughs are relatively stable as, for example, when the Cairngorm snows are melting at a nice steady pace throughout the spring and keeping the rivers at a good height, say 2–3ft, and relatively clear. Fish would be expected to take well at such a time. Conditions that are really bad news, almost as bad as a summer drought, are a rapid succession of high peaks and troughs. The water level, and the fish, never seem to settle. We might expect salmon to be 'gingered up', but experience shows that rapid rises and falls are not conducive to good fishing.

As the spate falls away and begins to clear, pausing fish can be taken in running and high-water lies. As the water falls further but still remains at a nice height on the gauge, the water clearing and the pools coming into ply, is when the majority of fish will be caught. Fisherman will find it rewarding to cover the pools at a good rate, seeking out the fish that are willing to take, rather than concentrating on a few small and clearly defined areas, although it will still be worth spending some time and particular attention on the pool tails and head-streams.

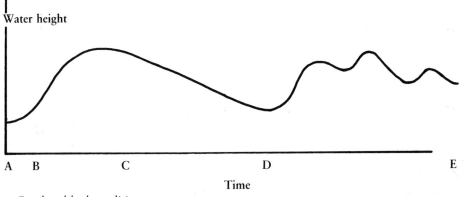

Good and bad conditions
A–B: Good at start of rise
B–C: Bad at height of spate
C–D: Good as water falls away
D–E: Bad as water rises and falls in unsettled fashion

Finally, we arrive at conditions of low water and the going is getting tough. Salmon have stopped running and sought out long-term, resident lies. Soon they will be as potted as the prawn or shrimp with which desperate fishermen are trying to tempt them.

Artificial water flows   What I have been speaking of are natural rises in water, caused by rain over the headwaters. Highland salmon fishermen, since the introduction of numerous hydro-electric schemes, have been of mixed opinions as to the value of artificial rises. There is certainly a case that they improve the fishing, but in what way?

Probably the most famous example of the effects of an artificial spate is that of the Grimersta. In late August 1888, an exceptionally dry summer had held up great quantities of salmon in the estuary. An artificial spate was created on the 22nd of the month and the fish ran in their thousands on the stale water from Loch Langabhat. Most fishermen are aware of the phenomenal catches that

Expert local advice on where fish will lie in a given height of water is invaluable

followed, but the point is this: these catches were made the following week, after it had started to rain. Until that time, although it was estimated that as many as ten thousand salmon and grilse had spread themselves over No 1 and No 2 lochs, only a handful were caught. There is certainly plenty of food for thought in this example.

Nature of pools As a final point in considering the height of water, it is important to realise that the pools on a river, indeed on a beat, are normally classified into high-water pools, low-water pools, or all-rounders capable of producing fish in a range of levels. It would be nice to say that these are easily recognisable, but often they are not, and it can take a number of seasons on one beat to discover which are which. I have already mentioned the small pool below my house that can produce a brace of fish as they start to run from the main holding pool below. It is not worth a cast in low water. And that little pool also points to the realisation that the best holding pools may not necessarily be the most productive.

Some things cannot be learnt from a book. The nature of the pools and where fish will take on a beat have to be learnt, very largely, by experience. This is where the services of a ghillie can be invaluable. Failing a full-time ghillie, the

Playing a salmon on the Spey. Note the high rod position (Arthur Oglesby)

A selection of flies and floating and sinking lines to see a salmon fisherman through most times and places (Arthur Oglesby)

advice of another fisherman who has fished the beat regularly should be treated as worth its weight in gold. On some beats, the estate factor or one of the keepers will happily give up an hour or two to walk the beat with any new fisherman and explain the nature of the pools and streams. Again, this is quite invaluable, so long as the man knows his subject. On Association water, local folk, if approached in the right way, are often surprisingly helpful in divulging information. Advice as to which pools fish best, and when, is far more important than the fact that 'auld Jock' had a nice fish of about 10lb on 'a wee hair-winged fly, kind of like a Blue Charm'.

TIME OF DAY AS A FACTOR

Beside the height of the water, the time of day can have a tremendous impact on the chances of finding a taking fish. Again, it is closely linked to the running characteristics of salmon.

A rise in water will set fish on the move but, as we have seen, for much of the time they are pausing or resting. This run, pause and rest pattern of behaviour is not haphazard. Salmon have a strong tendency to move at one particular time of day which varies with the seasons. Not that these are the only times of day at which they will run, but they are the times when the fisherman can look for maximum activity. By being aware of them, he will not make the mistake of sitting down to lunch or dinner, driving to the nearest town for supplies or simply going for a walk or taking a rest at the time when his chances of grassing a fish are at their peak.

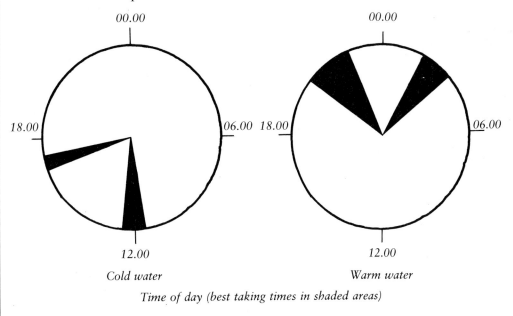

Cold water   Warm water

Time of day (best taking times in shaded areas)

From late spring to early autumn, say from toward the end of May until late September, most salmon movement occurs during the hours of darkness. It follows that, if given only two opportunities to fish the water, the fisherman should be wetting his flies during the last hours of daylight when salmon are moving out of their lies, and again at dawn when they are settling into new ones. Indeed, there is much to be said for the fisherman adopting a nocturnal habit in summer. Certainly, if I had access to a Spey beat in the main summer months, I would be strongly tempted to fish the last hours of daylight for salmon and grilse, then take up my sea trout rod until the first light of dawn returned the colour to the monochrome river, when I would switch my attentions back to salmon and grilse. Do people realise why their ghillies are bleary eyed when their guests arrive on the beat at 10 o'clock, or do they simply put it down to drink? Such are the thoughts that might be running through my mind at that time of day, as my head hit the pillow.

The salmon of the start and close of the season, in late winter and into early spring, and again in autumn, have a keener regard for the social niceties. They tend to move upstream at midday although, again, the final hour of daylight can produce fine sport and many a salmon has been netted from the Junction Pool at Kelso by the twinkling illumination of the street lights. The hours of daylight can be all too short for spring and autumn salmon fishing, just as they are for pheasant shooting. Why waste them on taking time off for a long lunch? Personally, I make do with a mug of soup in late morning, another in mid-afternoon and then spoil myself and my waistline when the light, and chances of sport, have completely faded away.

There is much talk nowadays of attempting to catch salmon at night. Certainly, in the summer months one would expect that, with fish running and pausing throughout the hours of darkness, they should be catchable. And yet, for all the time I spend fishing for sea trout at that time, I only take a very occasional and rare salmon when the night has really settled in. Theory may suggest otherwise, but experience shows that, in summer, dusk and dawn are the two main times to be wetting a fly for salmon.

SUMMING UP

Perfect conditions   It is, perhaps, a little unfair to suggest what I consider to be perfect fishing conditions. After all, they are so rarely encountered on the river bank, in fact the holiday fisherman may make many visits to a beat without enjoying their delight. However, it is different for those of us who live on the banks of a salmon river with plenty of alternatives within a relatively short drive, a network of friends to advise us of water levels, plus the ability, some of the time, to drop what we are doing and load the rods into the car.

Dusk and dawn are generally the best fishing times in summer

First, and most important, is the water height. I believe that this is absolutely fundamental to our chances of finding a taking fish. It is hard to catch the brief moment when fish 'come on the take' at the start of the rise; it may last for as little as half an hour. The spate must then run its course, and we cannot expect our chances to be good until the water has started to clear and fall, when we can try a cast over the high-water pools and lies. As the water continues to fall, salmon are running in greater numbers and the best chance is generally reckoned to be offered when the river has fallen to about one-third of the full height of the spate. In other words, following a 9ft rise above normal summer level, nothing would induce me to leave the river when it has fallen to about 3ft on the gauge.

Next, there is the time of day. As I have said, at the start and end of the season I would fish most confidently around midday, and again in the last of the light. In summer, it would be the few hours either side of, and including, dusk and dawn.

At other times   In what I have described as near perfect conditions I tend not to worry about other factors in the external and environmental stimuli to the fish but, at other times, I watch them more closely, seeking some sign that will make me fish with a little more hope and concentration.

At any height of water, time of day is still important. It has been suggested that light intensity is a factor in determining these times when, whatever the reason, even if the height of water is not conducive to salmon running, at least the urge to run is there. It is quite common for salmon to take a tour of the pool in the last of the light, and they may fall for a well-presented fly.

Salmon do not respond well at the extremes of temperature range but, in between, we are largely talking about how the air and water temperatures affect our tactics, rather than whether they affect our chances of finding a taking fish.

I suppose what we are looking for is some change in conditions, something to stimulate the fish. It might be a flash of sunlight on a dark and dreary day, but then again it could be a cloud passing over the sun on a bright day. In the dusk, a cold wind that has been blowing all day slowly fades and dies. Trout begin to rise. You develop a feeling for these things. A change is as good as a rest, they say, but for salmon it seems that many slight and subtle changes can effect their mood and, for however brief a time, they no longer want to rest. They are then vulnerable to the fisherman's fly once again.

3

THE SALMON FLY

The salmon fly has to be regarded as our most important item of tackle. It does not matter how large or small a fortune we spend on rods, reels, lines and other tackle so long as they are adequate for the job; it is the fly that the salmon accepts or rejects. Our chances of success depend strongly on this few shillings worth of hook, silk, fur and feather.

The size of fly seems to be the most important factor, and varies with water temperature and height as well as how we intend to fish the fly. The fisherman who seeks to pursue his sport throughout the season will need a range of sizes from the tiniest wisps to be used in high summer to much larger flies to be used in the cold conditions and high water encountered at the start and close of the season. And there is always a place, in my fly box at least, for a Collie Dog type of fly with its wing extending as much as 'quarter of a yard' behind the eye of the hook.

Next in importance comes the design of fly. Remember that in offering a caricature of a prey species to a salmon the behaviour of the fly, how it swims in the water, is just as important as its physical appearance. Design is not so much concerned with the size of the fly or the colours of its body, hackle and wing, but rather with its proportions, whether the wing is short or long and whether the fly is tied on a single hook, a double or a long-shanked treble, is a Waddington, wire body or tube, and whether that tube is plastic, aluminium or brass.

Then we come to the question of the actual pattern of fly, the colours and tones of the materials with which it is dressed. I do not believe that pattern is nearly as important as size or design, but that does not mean that I fall in with the modern, cavalier approach that says it has no bearing at all upon our success with salmon.

I suggested, when discussing the taking behaviour of salmon, that it is a mistake to consider the behaviour of the fish in terms of black and white, takers or non-takers. Many of the salmon to which we are presenting our fly may be teetering on the brink. They are suffering from conflicting stimuli, finely poised between the dominant, non-taking behaviour and disinhibition. Our fly has to tip the balance. To suggest that a change in size from a 6 to an 8 hook will make all the difference, but that the colours of the fly are totally irrelevant seems, somehow, illogical.

On a day of perfect conditions on a famous beat on a classic river, the fisherman is faced with a relatively easy situation. There are good numbers of salmon, a fair proportion of which may have swung, in terms of behaviour, into a state of disinhibition. The fisherman selects a good, general pattern of salmon fly and, at the end of the day, with six fish on the bank to write about, he feels justified in saying that pattern is unimportant, if not irrelevant. Does it enter his mind that he might, if he had spent a little more time in considering his choice of fly, have had seven or eight fish on the bank?

I am forever quoting the case of the copper-bodied fly that accounted for the record bag on the Downie Beat of the Beauly. Two men were fishing. One was catching fish on the copper fly, the other was catching nothing on another pattern of fly. Flies were swopped and the previously successful fisherman moved nothing while his companion, now armed with the copper fly, was soon into a fish. The fly was swopped back to its original owner, who went on to set the record for a single rod by lunchtime, when the remarkable little fly was lost, after which he caught nothing more. So is it any wonder that I keep a copper-bodied fly tucked away in my fly box?

In poor or marginal conditions, particularly on hard-fished Association water, a fisherman might fish all week and only encounter one or two salmon that were anything close to a disinhibited state. Size of fly and the speed, angle and depth of its presentation are all critical in influencing whether or not the fish may take and so, surely, even if to a far lesser extent, is the pattern of fly.

It was that marvellous fisherman, the late John Ashley Cooper, who suggested that the most important colours, those that seemed most attractive to salmon, are black, yellow and orange. Both the Willie Gunn and the Munro Killer combine all three, and they are very deadly patterns. Together, they probably account for nearly half of the fish that I catch.

However, the reason is fairly obvious. They are the patterns that I would naturally choose when a spate is running away, with the water clearing but still fairly high. As these are the most productive fly-fishing conditions on the river, it is little wonder that these two flies produce such a number of fish. Thus grows the legend of their killing powers.

But the point is that, simply because they are most suitable for that condition of water when most fish are caught, this does not imply that they are right for all conditions. I can think of various patterns of flies that I would prefer to use in, say, conditions of low water, high temperature and a bright sun or, at the other end of the scale, when the water is still running high and has not yet cleared.

The final 'body blow' used by those who say that they believe pattern is unimportant is to ask the simple question 'why?' I have no answer, any more than Baerends and Krujit could explain why those egg-rolling gulls showed a distinct preference for an oversized and bright-green egg. All I know is that, under certain conditions, I have found a given pattern of fly far more likely to be successful than another. This is not to say that I carry a host of patterns, but just that I prefer to carry at least four or five well-tried and proven patterns for general use, and a few others for special situations. But let me get back to the most important consideration in choosing a fly – its size.

With a good height of water and a stock of salmon, fly pattern may seem unimportant

SIZE OF FLY

If somebody was to ask why the pattern of fly is of any importance, my reply would be that I do not really know, but it is. Equally, I do not suppose that anybody can say why the size is so critical. As long as the fly is big in cold water, there seems to be little more to concern us; but why is it that, in higher temperatures, a change from an 8 to a 10 can make such a difference in gaining a response from fish?

One authority suggested it was because the salmon preyed on a certain species that differed in size with the temperature of the ocean current in which it was drifting. In other words, when the prey species was at its youngest and smallest, it was in fairly warm, southerly latitudes. As it drifted into ever colder climes, it was growing all the time. Apart from any other arguments that could be put against this hypothesis it would mean that, regardless of water speed and clarity, we should always fish the same size of fly. In warmer water, we do not. We find that best results come from increasing the size of fly as the water speed and height increase, and in reducing the size as the water flows gin clear. The Dee flows clearer than its near-neighbour the Spey, and many experienced fishermen who fish both these waters would agree that the Spey requires a slightly larger fly because of this.

Whatever theories we may come up with, salmon are always ready to show a few exceptions. Bill Currie in *Days and Nights of Game Fishing* has described a fish that I caught on the Aboyne water of the Dee at a time when soaring temperatures and low, clear water cried out for tiny flies. After two blank days fishing with size 12 Silver Stoats, I had only half an hour to go before making way for the next party of fishermen. I tied on an outrageous 1½in bright-yellow winged tube fly. Bill wrote:

> He said he watched it coming round in the water and thought how totally incongruous it looked in the low river. Well, you've guessed it. Halfway down a nice six-pounder took it – no messing about, a fine solid take with the hooks well in. It is nice to see one's guests getting fish, but isn't it the limit?

Of course, we cannot rewrite the books because of one or two such incidents that fly in the face of all our previous experiences. However there can be times when it pays to go from the sublime to the ridiculous. There are many things in salmon fishing, so many questions, to which we have not found definitive answers. We point to trends in behaviour, and base our tactics on the solid findings of generations of fishermen. But that should never prevent us from experimenting and introducing the occasional pinch of radical thought. The size of fly is very important, but even here there is room for flexibility in our choice.

Cold-water sizes   The salmon season starts in January on many rivers, and it is not uncommon for rivers to be frozen over at this time of year.

Salmon are not keen to enter the river if, as often happens in the opening months of the season, the river temperature is lower than that of the sea. When they do come up, they are lethargic and prefer deep, slow-water lies. The time of day at which they are likely to take is generally limited to a few hours either side of midday, with a second chance as the light wanes. Experience shows that salmon prefer a long fly at this time of year and, because they are lethargic, we must make an easy meal of our offering. A long fly, fished deep and slow: there lies the road to success in cold-water fishing, cold water being defined as between 32°F and 40°F.

When I say a 'long' fly, I mean something in excess of 2in, and I include the hook in that measurement. This should be emphasised, because there is often confusion as to what is meant. For example, the fisherman who chooses to tie his own flies may purchase a supply of 2in tubes. He then believes he is fishing with 2in flies. In my book, however, because he is then adding a treble hook at the tail, he is, to be precise, fishing a 2½in fly.

How long should we go? I think that a misconception has traditionally entered our thinking on cold-water fly sizes. Before the advent of modern tube flies in a variety of body materials ranging in weight from the lightest of plastic to the heaviest of brass, and the enormous significance of plastic fly lines in a full range of sinking rates, the fisherman had no choice but the standard fly, tied on a double or single hook, and the standard fly line of silk, which was not a very good tool for getting a fly down deep. In fact, those who still manufacture silk lines refer to them as neutral density, the equivalent of a modern plastic intermediate, the slowest of sinkers on offer.

At one time, the only change in tackle possible in order to fish the fly deeper was to increase the size of the fly. Therefore, when it was necessary to fish the fly deep in the coldest waters of spring and autumn, and particularly when the river was high, it was inevitable that the biggest flies were associated with such conditions. Fishermen, being a conservative lot, have maintained that association between depth and fly size. Personally, I am beginning to think that this may be a mistake. Of course I fish some really long flies, but as a result of technique and water speed when I feel that a fast fly may provoke the desired response, rather than because of water temperature for itself.

In the coldest water, everything possible is done to ensure that the fly fishes round as slowly as possible. I feel there is a possibility that, by using too long a fly, we run the risk of making the whole thing far too obvious. Therefore, in recent seasons I have been fishing mainly with 2in and 2½in flies in the coldest of water, and adjusting the depth at which the fly is fishing either by altering the sinking rate of the line or the body material of the fly. Having said that, I see body weight as an intrinsic part of fly design, having an enormous effect on how the fly fishes and how it responds to the vagaries of the stream.

Intermediate-temperature sizes From 40°F to 50°F may be considered as the intermediate temperature range, and it should bring a definite upswing in sport

Water temperature is very important in choosing an appropriate size of fly and deciding how it shall be fished

and what I regard as the cream of fishing with the sunk fly. The fish are no longer so lethargic and there will be far more of them entering the river as its temperature overtakes that of the sea.

Deep and slow is still the general rule. However, because it appears that there is no longer the need to fish quite so slowly, and fish are now moving out of the slowest water lies, it is possible to fish the fly rather faster and, therefore, to use a slightly larger one – sometimes a great deal larger. Salmon now seem prepared to move to a fly and have a stronger predatory response. I have enjoyed great sport, with water temperatures in the mid-forties, fishing a Collie Dog with its wing extending six or more tantalising and sinuous inches behind the eye of the hook. The aim is still to fish deep which requires quite a fast sinking line in streamier water but, by slightly increasing the angle of presentation, casting rather more squarely across the stream, and with gentle handlining across the slower stretches, this size and style of fly can be a strong stimulus to salmon.

As water temperatures climb into the upper forties, many fishermen suffer some anxiety as to what to do for the best. They are looking back on deep and slow tactics, and looking forward to smaller flies fished just below the surface, probably off a floating line. They itch to lay aside their sinking lines and be on with the much more pleasant task of casting a floater. Many will resort to some sort of intermediary tactic, a halfway house between conventional sunk and floating-line techniques, and thousands of words have been written for and against 'midwater tactics' which largely rely on fishing a heavy fly off a floater, or a lighter but similar size of fly off a medium sinking or sink-tip line.

In water temperatures around the upper forties, a salmon may be prepared to accept all manner of offerings. Normally, I have found that the greatest success comes from fishing a biggish fly quite quickly off a fast sinking line in the streamier parts of the pool, and I generally stick to these tactics until the water temperature has steadied into the fifties. However, this is one of those situations, of which there are so many in salmon fishing, where it is foolish to make any hard and fast rules. Splendid sport may be enjoyed with a 1½in or 2in fly on an aluminium or copper tube, or the lighter of the wire-bodied flies, fished off an intermediate line. And, when the air temperature is a few degrees or more higher than that of the water – vital if the salmon are going to show any great degree of interest in a fly swimming just below the surface – either a light plastic tube fished off an intermediate, or a double-hooked fly fished off a floater, can be very productive. The fly might very well be something like a Munro Killer tied on a size 4 hook, with its wing extending to 1½ times the length of the body.

Warm-water sizes   I have never been able to discover why 48°F was accepted as the changeover point between large salmon flies being fished deep and smaller flies being fished just below the surface. It implies that, at a given moment, all salmon experience some sort of metamorphosis. It ignores the fact that for many days and weeks, the water temperature may be rising and falling above and below this point.

In spring, I like to wait until the water temperature has steadied in the fifties before giving up the large and deep salmon fly although, as I have said, I make no hard and fast rules about this, particularly at about noon when there is a blink of sun about. In autumn, on the other hand, I am reluctant to lay aside the smaller fly fished just below the surface until the temperature of the water has dropped below 45°F. Ignoring the finer points, it seems certain that, in general, salmon show a marked preference for the smaller range of fly sizes when the water temperatures are in or beyond the fifties.

And here the fishing theorists have an absolute field-day, with those tables purporting to show exactly which size of fly to use. First measure the water temperature, then examine its speed, height and clarity, feed all these facts into a riverside computer, mutter the magic words and hey presto! It all sounds marvellous, and obviously has great appeal to inexperienced fishermen but, when we remember the complexities of predicting whether or not a salmon will take and the possibilities and permutations of internal and external stimuli, does it still seem appropriate to suggest that it is possible to predict when a salmon is likely to prefer a size 8 to a 6 or, as some theorists will go as far to suggest, an 8 to a 7?

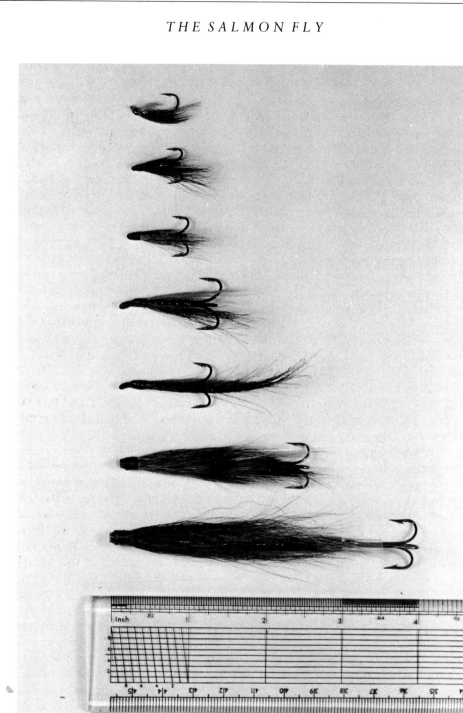

Throughout the long season, a fisherman will use a full range of fly sizes

However, we should not snigger because the majority of us think in that way. My own attitude is to acknowledge that salmon prefer an ever smaller fly as temperature increases, but I am not prepared to pretend for one moment that I can predict exactly what size of fly will induce a salmon to seize it. Salmon are not simply machines all reacting identically to some pre-set programme. We are back to general trends of salmon behaviour, the possibilities and probabilities of a sport in which there are few definitive statements. Therefore, I can say no more than that, in temperatures of 50–55°F, I regard a size 6 or the equivalent length of tube as the standard size, with sizes 4 and 8 as logical possibilities. And I may fish with a longer fly; certainly one with a long wing in which, although the hook employed may be a size 6, the overall length of the fly is closer to a size 2. From 55–60°F water temperature, a size 8 becomes my standard, with sizes 6, 10 and the long-winged derivatives as its sidekicks. Up to 65°F, I think in terms of sizes 10, 8 and 12.

When temperatures soar in excess of 65°F, life becomes very difficult for the salmon, due to the ever decreasing level of oxygen. My own thoughts turn to reading a good book in some shady spot, cool drink to hand, throughout the daylight hours, although I may try a tiny wisp of a tube fly, armed with a minute treble. I really do mean tiny – barely any body at all behind the head, and a size 14 treble. I much prefer to wait for the hours of dusk and dawn when I try a similar or rather larger fly in the rapid streams in the neck of holding pools where salmon come to drink in the oxygen of the aerated streamy and broken water, as well as responding to the urge to run that comes with each and every dusk of the summer months.

Water-speed factor   The important factor in deciding which fly size to use for a given temperature range is the water speed. This speed can be considered in two quite distinct ways. Firstly, we can take a passive attitude and say that it is simply a matter of estimating the speed of the current. For the majority of fishermen this may be sufficient, because they simply cast out their fly and let it fish round. They do little to alter the angle at which they cast and would not dream of handlining. However, even then, they are ignoring the fact that the fly may, for example, be fishing through two streams divided by relatively still water; fishing through two sections of water flowing at 6mph and three sections at 3mph. In order to maintain the same water speed, a fly hanging stationary in a 6mph current must swim into a 3mph current at 3mph or into a 4mph current at 2mph.

We know from practical experience that, as we increase the water speed of the fly, we must also increase the fly size and, conversely, we can reduce the size of the fly as its speed is reduced. Looking at the lowest of the warm-water temperature ranges, from 50–55°F, a size 6 is regarded as the standard size, to be fished in a medium paced stream. In a faster stream, I would go for a size 4; or even bigger if the water were high and flowing really fast; and if it were a fairly sluggish stream, first choice would be the 8, as often as not. Water speed is also affected by the angle at which we cast. The general rule is that, the squarer we cast, the faster the fly swims across.

How does water speed affect practical fishing technique and tackle? When faced with a pool containing a host of varied paces of current from the full force of the stream in the neck, slowly decelerating into the body before gaining momentum and accelerating through the glide and into the tail, my own approach is to start with the biggest size indicated, being the fly that seems appropriate to the fastest part of the pool, normally in the headstream. This is where the fly will have to be fished slowly, reducing its water speed to as close as possible to the speed of the current. This is done with a shallow angled cast. This angle increases further down the pool, speeding the passage of the fly but, because the current speed is decreasing, maintaining the original water speed. In the body of the pool, the cast will be comparatively square. As the current increases toward the tail, the angle of cast becomes ever shallower until it has reverted to that used in the neck.

We can also alter our tactics to create subtle differences in the type of stimulus that we present to an individual fish. For example, let us imagine that we have seen a fish from some observation point, or that a fish has moved to our fly without making firm contact and, having rested him for a time, we are returning to try for him again. With the small, medium and large flies possible within the temperature bracket, we can logically offer the fish in a known position three alternatives. First, with a squarish cast, and possibly introducing controlled drag, we obtain maximum water speed and therefore use the large fly. Next, we can wade further across the stream and, casting at about 45 degrees, offer the medium size. If that does not work, we can try the smallest fly, reducing its water speed as far as possible by wading out still further and casting a long line at a shallow angle.

Equally, if we are deep wading to begin with, we can reverse the above tactics, reducing the size of fly as we move downstream and toward the bank, going as far as to use a really long fly, cast almost upstream and pulled across with the belly of the line as a last ditch effort.

Such tactics can be used in various forms when fishing a pool, rather than simply to an individual fish. On those long and productive pools of the Spey and similar waters, we could try first time down with a large fly, fished from a line running quite parallel but close to the shore, and cast quite squarely. Second time down, we might get in really deep, wetting the tops of our chest waders, and use a smaller fly at a shallower angle and slower speed.

A flexible approach   We can only talk in terms of general trends in salmon behaviour, and the suggestions made in regard to fly size should, therefore, be considered only as general recommendations. The range in size in regard to water temperature and speed is flexible. Generally, in salmon fishing, we do all we can to fish the fly as slowly as possible, but there are days when this approach does not produce the goods, and these are the times when it may pay to vary

We can only talk in terms of general trends when interpreting success

from the sublime to the ridiculous. I have had too much sport on flies of 2in in length, sometimes longer, fished fast across rapid streams even with water temperatures well up in the sixties, to suggest otherwise. Nowadays, I largely depend on one specific type of fly for this style of fishing, and that leads us into fly design and pattern.

DESIGN OF FLY

It is not enough that a salmon fly should look right; it should also behave correctly. For example, there seems no logic at all in a fly that does not swim on an even keel. Also, a fly that is able to respond to the vagaries of the stream, darting here and hovering there, rising and falling, must have a far greater semblance of life than a heavy, stolid fly.

When I was a lot younger and attending HMS Conway, a naval cadet school, they taught us all about weight to surface area ratios in regard to the design of boats and ships. Sad to say, I have forgotten the more intimate details. What I do remember is that, as you increase the surface area in proportion to the weight, you increase the buoyancy. This is not the place to start discussing displacement

Spinning and wobbling lures are obvious representations of prey fish but, with flies, the similarities are more subtle

– you don't need me to tell you that a large object weighing the same weight as a small object may float, while the smaller object may sink. And you may not be interested in the reasons why a steel or concrete boat doesn't sink to Davy Jones's locker; but it is an important point when we come to look at long-tailed flies which increase the surface area to weight ratio, and when we are thinking of how certain body materials will effect the swimming action of the fly.

Cold-water flies   Generations of fishermen have rediscovered the truth that, in cold-water conditions up to 50°F, the salmon is most likely to respond to a large, or rather long, fly; something in excess of 2in. Over that temperature, they probably require something a lot smaller, although the long fly can and does still score.

I do not intend to consider the development of the design of the cold-water salmon fly any further back than the day that Richard Waddington bent a piece of wire into an eyed shank, attached a treble hook, and launched the articulated fly onto the fishing scene. He may not have been the first to use this type of fly design, but he certainly publicised and popularised its use. Before that, we were dealing with little more than overgrown trout flies, delightful to the eye and quite capable of catching a certain amount of fish, but a never ending source of argument as to whether, in a wing composed of possibly a dozen separate and clearly defined feathers, a strip of Toucan feather could be substituted for Indian Crow. In those days a man would sit in a fireside armchair using a magnifying glass to check that his flies, beautiful little gems of the fly dresser's art, had been tied to exactly the correct proportions. But, just as a 4½ litre super-charged Bentley of the thirties is no longer likely to win the Monaco Grand Prix, so salmon flies have moved on into a new era of logical design and efficiency.

Although I have already devoted a section to the size of salmon fly, I must mention it again as it affects closely the design of fly. Richard Waddington insisted that it was totally wrong to use a fly of less than 3in in cold-water conditions. To an extent, I would agree with him. However, when the water is barely hovering above freezing point and the fish that come nosing up into the lower pools are very lethargic, slow to respond and seek out the slower, deeper water, we must fish our fly deep and very slow. Deep and slow, that is the way to fish in cold water, serving up our offering on a plate. What we must realise is that we are giving the salmon all the time in the world to inspect, reject or accept

Traditional salmon fly   *Tube fly*

the fly. But our caricature must not be too visible or all too obviously a fake, therefore, in these coldest of water conditions, I prefer to fish with the smallest possible flies within the class, that is flies of 2 or 2½in.

Having rejected the possibilities of big single or double hooks, because they simply do not hook or hold as well as articulated flies armed with a treble hook, that leaves us with tube flies, Waddington shanks and the wire-bodied Brora style flies.

Looking firstly at tube flies, we have the alternatives of heavy, medium and light in the form of brass, aluminium and plastic tubes. For reasons described in the chapters on fishing tactics, I do not like the heavy fly. I far prefer to fish a faster sinking line with a lighter fly in order to achieve the same depth. The lighter fly, being more active in the water, is more attractive to salmon and the weight of the treble hook, which tends to pull a light tube down at the tail, is counteracted by the downward pull of the fast sinking line at the head. For these reasons, brass tubes have little if any part to play in my fishing. Aluminium is my first choice in tubes, with plastic in reserve for the very slowest of stretches; but neither of these will ever threaten my allegiance to the Waddingtons and wire-bodied Brora design.

The single-shank Waddington could easily be the basis of tremendous salmon flies. It is not. I have spoken to the manufacturers, but they do not seem to understand that, by tapering the shank toward the head and leaving so much excess weight in the tail, they create a fly that is bound to be pulled down at the tail so that it is impossible to expect the fly to fish on an even keel. A good shank should be made in the shape of a dart, with the weight toward the head and tapering away toward the tail. If, in addition, these shanks were offered in light, medium and not too heavy versions, I for one would use them exclusively for this class of fishing.

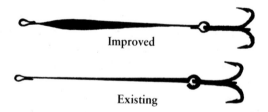

Single Waddington shank: if the shank was re-designed as shown,
to the shape of the dart, it would be greatly improved

That leaves us with the other form of Waddington shank – the double, formed from a continuous loop of wire broken only at one point, a little above the tail, in order that a treble hook can be added. These, like the plastic tubes, I find are rather too light for most fishing situations although, again, I do use them in the very slowest stretches of water.

Other than that, we have the Brora flies, and these are now my firm favourites.

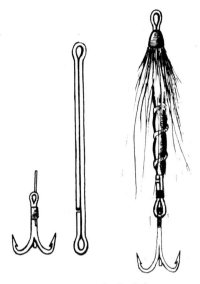

'Brora' wire-bodied fly

Basically, they are nothing more than a rather heavier version of the double Waddington shank. Rob Wilson, who owned the tackle shop in Fountain Square, Brora, made up these shanks in stainless steel, and fishermen on the highly productive salmon rivers of the north-east were quick to realise their virtues. Personally, I make them up on copper wire, salvaged from the local scrap yard. By varying the thickness of the wire, it is possible to vary the weight of the fly.

The Rob Wilson, extra-strong, outpoint trebles produced by Partridge, the hook manufacturers, are regarded by many experienced salmon fishermen as the ultimate weapon for cold-water salmon fishing. The treble is held in alignment with a stiff length of nylon whipped to both hook and body shank, but is still free to move and eliminate leverage on the hold when a fish is hooked. They cast well and swim superbly. Since the break, the gap upon which the treble is added to the shank, is placed as close as possible to the tail as is done in the double Waddington, it is a simple matter to replace a damaged hook.

These are the flies that I use for much of my cold-water fishing. Indeed, the only occasion when I use any other design in what are traditionally considered the 'sunk line' times of the season, is when I want to fish a fly in excess of about 3½in, including the treble hook.

Why not simply fish a longer Brora? More to the point, why fish with a longer fly at all? To answer the last question first; while it is a relatively simple matter to fix a minimum length for cold-water salmon flies, recent experiences are leading many fishermen to question what is the maximum. Fish are now being caught on flies described as 'quarter of a yard' long, a nice way to express 9in. And such

In choosing a fly, we should think of how it will swim as well as what it looks like

flies, in a certain design, can provoke a strong and apparently predatory response from salmon.

I associate these very long flies with cold-water conditions, but normally not until the temperature has risen to about 40°F and upwards. Fish are no longer anything like as lethargic as they were when the temperature was down in the thirties; they have moved into rather streamier water and they are prepared to make more of an effort to sieze a fly. The first reason why Broras, or any articulated fly where the body reaches the full length of the fly, is unlikely to be suitable – besides considerations of casting such an air-resistant brute – are that they would be far too obviously a caricature. True, we might try fixing the treble at the end of a long length of undressed and practically invisible plastic tube. However, we really don't want the fly at the tail of such long dressings; we want it quite close to the head.

Forget all those stories about keeping the wing within the body length of the fly, all those tales of how a salmon will nip at a trailing wing. With these long flies, it simply isn't so. Tie a long, trailing hair wing to a single salmon hook, say a size 1, forget about a body or hackle, and you have a fly that will catch many a salmon for you. But why is it that they do not simply nip at the tail?

When a sea bird, or even a kingfisher, is seen to catch a fairly large fish, it can be observed that the bird, before swallowing, will normally turn the fish so that it enters its throat head first. If it did not do this, the fish's fins and scales would stick, just like smoothing feathers the right way and then the wrong way. It seems that predatory fish go one stage better. They know to catch smaller prey fish by the head, or certainly by the front part of the body. Sea anglers are well aware of this. When they go fishing for pollack, bass or even mackerel, using natural sand-eels, they know that the right place for the hook is not far behind the sand-eel's gill covers. There is hardly as much as 2in of sand-eel in front of the hook and probably 7 or 9in trailing behind. And very rarely, if ever, is the tail-piece chopped off, certainly not by the quarry fish.

And when they travel further afield in search of the mighty predators of the sea such as the blue marlin, it is recognised that when trailing a Kona Head lure, the most effective lures for this species, the target area is the head. That is where the hook is placed, rather than back in the trailing plastic skirt. And the same is just as true when they use a Knucklehead or plastic skirt over natural bait for white marlin, or Japanese feathers for tuna. Enough of that. We've dipped our toes in the waters of the Caribbean, the Barrier Reef and the Azores; time to get back to the salmon river.

Looking closer at the design of these enormously long salmon flies, the most common example is the Collie Dog. The collie dog that works sheep and cattle, rather than the one we fish with, has long, trailing feathers of hair on its hind legs. It is marvellous hair with just the right texture and wave in it to produce a fly wing that will swim superbly in streamy water. However, it must be pointed out that while you are attacking the collie's back leg with a pair of scissors, he is more than well equipped at t'other end to make his complaint felt! There are a number of other possibilities, such as the tails of black cattle, although these are often frayed at the ends after seasons of fly-switching. A raven-haired girl, deciding on a change to a short hair-style, will be surprised to realise the number of admirers she has suddenly gained.

In the original Collie Dog, the hair was simply lashed to a single hook of about size 1, and this still works well. However, remembering what was said earlier about surface area to weight ratios, this can produce a fly that is just a bit too

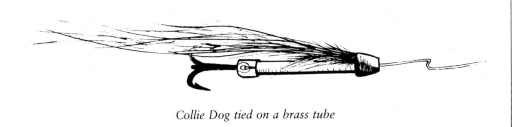

Collie Dog tied on a brass tube

lively and buoyant. This is one of the few occasions when I use a brass tube. The fly may have to cut down through a heavy push of water and, while we want the Collie to fish with the semblance of life, that does not mean we need it to be darting about like a demented bumble bee on heat. Generally, a 1–1½in brass tube is about right. Other than whipping on the hair, all that needs to be added is a length of flexible extension tubing to hold the outpoint treble hook in place, a size 6. If the bare body of the tube offends you, cover its nakedness with silver or gold Mylar tube, which can be said to accentuate the target area of the front of the fly. And there we have the Collie Dog – a totally logical and, at times, ever so deadly pattern of fly to present to salmon. Incidentally, try the silver Mylar-bodied Collie on fresh-run sea trout, still close in memory to chasing sand-eels in coastal waters.

Warm-water flies   In terms of tackle and techniques, the watershed in salmon fishing occurs at about 50°F. Salmon are now prepared to raise themselves to a smaller fly fishing just below the surface of the water. Equally, they are showing a marked preference for lies in faster, streamier and generally shallower water.

There are at least two possibilities to achieve the shallow depth of fly that is now required. One method is to fish a very light fly off an intermediate or slow sinking line. This offers a very lively fly and one that may be best suited to fishing the rather slower stretches of water. In faster streams, there is sufficient life in the current for me to have no doubts whatsoever in fishing a slightly heavier fly below a floating line.

Returning to the light-fly, intermediate-line combination, it must be emphasised that the intention is for the fly to fish above the level of the line. I have christened this 'the balloon effect', likening it to a small child holding a balloon at the end of a piece of string. The balloon rises, darts and hovers above the child, just as the light fly plays above the line, tethered to it by a length of monofilament. The best design of fly for this work is a plastic-bodied tube fly, armed with an outpoint treble. I carry such flies in a range of sizes from just over 1in long, equivalent to a size 4, down to the tiniest wisps of a tube, with hardly any body behind the head, armed with a minute but deadly size 16 treble. If any of these flies are dropped onto water they will, quite literally, float, even when the treble hook is in place.

These flies are, of course, tail heavy and therefore totally unsuitable for use with a floating line. Beside the fact that they would skid across the surface, the floating line would pull them even further up at the head, and push down the tail even more. There is one time when they can be used with the floating line, however, namely when we seek to riffle a fly in the surface film (see page 124).

For the more conventional fly to be fished off a floating line, there are quite a few possibilities. I believe the Americans still use single hooks to a certain degree but, quite honestly, I cannot remember the last time I saw one in use on a British river, although I have no doubt that they still have a few die-hard supporters. Today, I hardly think of using a single hook, unless I am fishing with a dropper.

Standard and low-water doubles: designated as the same size, this refers to the gape, not the length of the hook

That leaves us with standard and low-water, slightly longer, doubles; long-shanked and extra long-shanked trebles; Waddingtons, Broras and various metal-bodied tube flies. I use them all, but will start by considering the doubles.

I should say that the standard double catches the great majority of summer salmon and grilse on the floating line in warm-water conditions. It is the traditional favourite. A fisherman armed with nothing but standard double-hook flies would have very little to worry about. If there is any advantage to the low-water double it is that, for the same size of gape, it is rather longer; put another way, a size 6 low-water is about the same length as a size 4 standard. This means that we can reduce or increase the surface area to weight ratio if we please, and the lighter low-water hook will swim that little bit closer to the surface and be that little bit more lively. One of the objections to the low-water is that it increases the leverage on the hook-hold but, while I accept this is a problem with single hooks, I have no worries in this regard when fishing the double, simply because of my own experience with this style of hook.

So, we might choose to fish standard doubles in the stronger streams and low-waters in the slightly gentler flows. But we cannot leave it there because silver-bodied, streamer like, long-winged flies such as the Bourrach and Kenny's Killer, both tied on low-water hooks, are such excellent flies for tempting grilse in the fastest of streams. It is far from scientific, but somehow no long-winged fly looks quite right on a standard length hook. And if it doesn't look right, how can I or anybody else be expected to fish it with confidence? And it is not just the silver-bodied flies that make up into good long-winged flies; even the Munro Killer can be very productive in this style.

As a general guide use long wings on low-water hooks, to create a light and lively fly with a high surface area to weight ratio, a fly that can prove equally effective off an intermediate line in the faster flows. When fishing fast, streamy water with the floating line, however, we want a fly that will settle down in the water, and a fly having the normal length of wing and tied on a standard double will normally be first choice.

Practically the same comments that have been made in regard to doubles can be applied to trebles where the fly is dressed directly onto the hook. Colonel Esmond Drury introduced the long-shanked treble in competition to the standard double hook and, in the intervening seasons, more and more fishermen have answered the question 'you wouldn't fish with a treble with one of the

*Esmond Drury trebles: marvellous
hookers and holders of fish*

hooks broken off, would you?' and discovered its tremendous hooking and holding power. In later years, Partridge introduced the extra-long shanked treble. These make up into deadly, slim-profile flies – like a very thin tube fly – in contrast to the more dumpy lines of the Drury hook, and I use them a lot.

For those who cannot help worrying about leverage, the shorter Waddington shanks armed with a separate and tiny treble hook offer the same slim profile as the extra-long shanked treble and give another light and lively fly, possibly best considered in conjunction with intermediate lines in faster streams.

Then there is the wire-bodied Brora. This gives us a slim profile, but with a little extra weight. I have been using these flies rather a lot in recent seasons, particularly in a good height of water, with the temperature barely over 50°F on larger rivers such as the Spey. It is hard to make them up with a body length of less than 1in but, when conditions demand the larger size of fly to be fished off a floating line, these flies are even better than the standard double for settling down in the water and fishing well.

Finally, there are the metal-bodied tube flies. I hope that the implications of their various weights are obvious. For example, in the circumstances that I have just outlined for fishing one of the smaller Brora flies off a floating line, an aluminium tube would prove just as effective. And there are times in high summer when a tiny fly tied on a brass tube can tempt the 'sulky boys'. However, on the whole, I wonder whether the metal tubes are just a little bit too dumpy when encountered in any length less than about 1in and so, except for the cases mentioned, I rarely use them.

PATTERNS OF FLY

Cold-water flies   The pattern of the Collie Dog has been fully described, except to note that black hair usually seems to work best. In regard to the other classes of cold-water flies, be they tubes, Waddingtons or those marvellous Broras, I stick to variants upon the general theme of the Willie Gunn.

The standard Willie Gunn has a black body, ribbed with oval gold tinsel. The wing is made up of equal parts of black, orange and yellow hair. Opinions differ as to whether this hair, probably either goat or bucktail, should be mixed before it is tied in. Personally, I like to tie my Willie Gunns with black over orange over yellow wings.

By using a tinsel rib we may be adding some flash to the fly but, more importantly, we are breaking up the long line of the body, making it that little bit less obvious. Equally, by using three colours of hair in the wing, we are avoiding a solid outline. It used to be said that the golden pheasant topping laid along the tops of traditional salmon-fly wings shimmered and broke up the harsh outline of the wing.

The variants on the Willie Gunn come about by altering the proportion of the colours of hair in the wing. For example, for use in coloured water, a fly with yellow over orange hair, the outline broken only by a few strands of black, is very effective. For clear water, a wing that is practically all black, with just a few strands of orange over yellow beneath can be equally attractive.

I carry two other slightly different flies. Other than black, orange and yellow, red can often provoke a response. Therefore, I have a fly with a red body and a wing in which the standard colours are reduced to allow an equal proportion of red hair. The other fly is a variant on the theme of the White Wing – a sort of White Wing-Willie Gunn cross. It has a black body ribbed with silver and the wing is roughly one-third yellow under two-thirds white, with a few strands of black overall. This fly also incorporates Jungle cock cheeks and therefore, in order to ensure that it swims with the cheeks at the sides, I gently upturn the eye of a Brora shank with a pair of pliers. On the manufactured Waddington shanks, this refinement is already added. Does it make any difference to the fish? I haven't a clue, but it makes me fish more confidently. It is a fly that works well in the fading light of an early season dusk.

Warm-water flies   The following list is intended as a ready reference to some of the flies on which I have enjoyed sport, together with suggestions as to when and where I might choose to use them. There is no need to carry them all at once. For example, if fishing the Spey in the peak of the floating-line time, I would be more than happy with a range of sizes of Munro Killers; Grey, Blue and Yellow Squirrel; a Bourrach and a Black Maria. Equally, my Copper Orange normally only gets used when fish are running on high water, still bearing a touch of colour. And the Kenny's Killer is really a grilse fly, at least for me. However, put together, they offer a reasonable selection of warm-water flies and, with them, I would be happy to visit practically any river where the Atlantic salmon run.

ARNDILLY FANCY

Tag: oval silver
Tail: golden pheasant crest
Body: yellow floss
Rib: oval silver
Hackle: bright blue

Wing: black
Cheeks: Jungle cock
Head: front two-thirds red, remainder black

COMMENT: Many years ago, a ghillie told me that a black-and-yellow fly was a firm favourite on his beat of the Spey. The Arndilly is, like the Black Maria, just such a fly and a firm favourite on days with some sunshine. A fly that I associate with one of the most famous fly-tying professionals, Megan Boyd of Kintardwell, it is as attractive to the fisherman's eye as it is deadly to the salmon.

BLACK BRAHAN

Tag: oval silver
Body: red lurex
Rib: oval silver

Hackle: black
Wing: black

COMMENT: A straightforward fly that can prove particularly useful for salmon and grilse at dawn and dusk. A good variant differs only in that it has a green lurex body.

BLACK MARIA

Tag: oval silver
Tail: golden pheasant crest
Body: rear half, yellow; front half, black floss

Rib: oval silver
Hackle: black
Wing: black

COMMENT: Another of the black-and-yellow flies that can prove so successful on the Spey. It is reported that 500 salmon fell to this fly in one season at Knockando.

BOURRACH

Tag: oval silver
Tail: blue hackle-point
Body: flat silver

Rib: oval silver
Hackle: blue
Wing: yellow

COMMENT: A slim, shimmering streak of yellow in the water and quite excellent for fishing fast, broken streams in bright conditions. Very definitely a fly to be tied in the long-winged style, on the slimmer profile hooks, or shanks.

COPPER ORANGE

Tag: oval gold
Body: copper lurex
Rib: oval gold
Hackle: orange

Wing: orange, from the part of the bucktail that would be brown in the natural, undyed tail
Head: red

COMMENT: Other than the Shrimp Fly, this is my only fly that includes a red head. All my others are finished in black, except the half-coloured Arndilly Fancy. Like the Bourrach, very definitely a long-wing pattern. I made this one up specifically for those occasions when a late summer spate sets resident fish on the move. I like to think there is something about the colour that brings out an aggressive response but, whatever the reasons for its success, it has proved a very useful pattern in high water.

GREY, BLUE AND YELLOW SQUIRREL

Tag: oval silver
Tail: golden pheasant crest
Body: black floss
Rib: oval silver

Hackle: yellow under blue guinea-fowl
Wing: grey squirrel over blue over yellow

COMMENT: A fly called the Grey Squirrel is particularly popular on the Annan, a river near my home. However, I have been so impressed with the performance of such tricolour flies as the Munro Killer, that I made up this variant at my fly bench. I have not been disappointed at the results and regard it as an excellent pattern for fairly low, clear-water conditions and anytime when there is more than a blink of sunlight.

HAIRY MARY

Tag: oval gold
Tail: golden pheasant crest
Body: black floss

Rib: oval gold
Hackle: medium blue
Wing: brown

COMMENT: One of the earliest patterns of hair-winged flies to be widely adopted in this country. There are many alternative dressings, but I believe this to be the 'correct' one. A fly that conjures up images of the rivers and lochs of the Hebrides and western seaboard.

KENNY'S KILLER (GOLD)

Tag: oval gold
Tail: golden pheasant tippet
Body: flat gold

Rib: oval gold
Hackle: yellow
Wing: black

COMMENT: I can only hope that Ken Burns will forgive me for exchanging the silver body of his original Killer for one of gold. My only excuse is that I already carry a silver-bodied Bourrach, and there are times when the softer gold body works well in this long-winged fly. Having said that, the silver-bodied Kenny's Killer is an excellent fly in the smaller sizes for summer salmon and grilse in bright weather and low, clear water.

MUNRO KILLER

Tag: oval gold
Body: black floss
Rib: oval gold

Hackle: orange under blue guinea-fowl
Wing: black over orange over yellow

COMMENT: Quite probably the most successful of the modern generation of salmon flies, together with its big brother the Willie Gunn. Like any well-known and enormously successful fly, it is subject to a host of variations in dressing, but this is the one I now prefer, and I would not travel without it. It is rather similar to the traditional Thunder and Lightning in some ways and, like that fly, is deadly on rivers that are naturally dark or when a spate is running off on any river. If limited to one pattern of fly, this would be it because it is so suitable for those times when the majority of fish are likely to be caught.

SHRIMP FLY

Tag: oval gold
Tail Hackle: golden pheasant red breast-feather, pointing to the rear
Body: rear-half yellow floss with oval-gold rib
Centre Hackle: orange cock

Body: front-half black floss ribbed oval silver
Front Hackle: badger cock
Cheeks: Jungle cock
Head: red

COMMENT: Ireland must surely be recognised as the home of the Shrimp Fly, of which there are a number of variations. This particular Shrimp is the pattern tied by that great professional Jimmy Younger. Another good pattern is Curry's Red. It is a good fly to try anywhere during the summer months, but I find it particularly useful on smaller rivers where it can provoke a strong response if fished with a slow sink-and-draw. In Ireland, the Shrimp Flies are great favourites for spring salmon fishing on such waters as Lough Beltra. I invariably tie this fly on a standard double hook.

Final comments   If you don't tie your own flies; why not? There are certainly worse vices at which to while away the closed season. And, by tying your own flies, you are able to design them, alter the proportions, and introduce all sorts of subtleties into the finished pattern.

Incidentally, for the more technically minded, I always use black tying silk on my salmon flies and I have the utmost faith in Partridge hooks. The heads are finished with one coat of thin Cellire varnish which is given a couple of days to really dry and harden before completing the head with Humbrol Enamel.

4

TACKLE

It is said that a good workman never blames his tools. It might be better to say that a good workman will not tolerate any tools that are not beyond reproach. I have heard arguments as to whether salmon fishing is an art or a science; it is above all, a craft. And just as the skilled woodworker cannot bring out the figure and texture of his materials without the right range of tools, so the salmon fisherman cannot do justice to his knowledge of the fish unless he has the right tools and can use them to their full advantage.

If you put two fishermen on a beat, both having roughly the same degree of experience, it will assuredly be the one with the most suitable tackle and greatest ability to use it who will encounter success. I remember reading how, at the turn of the century, when fishermen on the Ness had tried for a salmon but were unable to cover it or, more likely, cover it properly, they would send for Alexander Grant. Known as the 'wizard of the Ness', here was a man who could cast to, and hook, salmon at 50yd range – a tremendous feat. One wonders what his achievements might have been in the modern age. Would he have fished any better with modern plastic lines rather than his square-plait silk, and what would the man who invented the greenheart Grant Vibration rod have made of carbon fibre? We shall never know.

Talking to ghillies and fishermen who knew him, the late John Ashley Cooper was very probably the greatest salmon fisherman of modern times. Casting in all sorts of conditions, his performance was far and above that of the common man. I spoke to him of the tackle he used, and realised the thought that had gone into its choice. There was simply no room in his thinking or tackle box for equipment that did not meet the high and thoroughly practical standards he set.

When we think of salmon tackle, thoughts automatically turn to rods but, because it is the first link in the chain between fly and fisherman, let's start with some thoughts on leaders.

LEADERS

The leader is nothing more than a length of monofilament nylon that acts as a link between the fly and the casting line; or is it? Certainly the tale is told of the Tweed fisherman who tied his fly directly to the main line, and caught a fish on it; but such stories serve only as amusing tales and do not detract from the fact that the length and breaking strain, or rather thickness, of the leader material play a material part in deciding how our fly will fish.

Nylon leaders can be abraded on rocky, boulder-strewn rivers

There is little sense in using nylon that is not as strong as possible, so long as it is suitable for use with our chosen size of fly. On the other hand, we need not fear using fairly light nylon if we have to, when fishing tiny flies which could not work and swim naturally on heavier quality. Don't expect a feather to float in a breeze if it is attached to a heavy length of rope.

Probably the greatest strain placed on the leader, and tackle in general, is when a heavy fish has been fought to a standstill and is coming up on its side when it is still in fast, streamy water. If you have ever hooked a discarded plastic fertiliser sack, you will know the dogged fight it can put up with only its surface area and the force of the current to help it. You are having to tow a dead weight, and it comes down to little more than a tug-of-war straining everything to its limits. Where the current is strong, and particularly where the fish run large, strong leaders are a must. The other day I was talking to a fisherman who had just returned from Norway. He told me of fish that he had caught on the fly and

Blyth Oxley with a Spey salmon of 38lb; what a tragedy if such a fish were lost due to unsound tackle

of another that he had to break in, when it was carried away by the full force of the heavy stream.

Any person who has fished such a river as the Kirkaig in western Sutherland will know the rock-strewn nature of its short pools and cascades. On such rivers the nylon can easily be abraded on rocks as a fish is being played, and again it would be foolish to fish with anything but strong nylon.

Another important point to remember is that, if you choose to overhead cast, your fly will be travelling at the speed of a bullet as it reaches the extent of the back cast. A large and heavy fly, coming to an abrupt stop, can easily snap light nylon or certainly weaken it.

So, what nylon should be carried? I would suggest that for all flies within the class of cold-water designs, flies of more than 2in length, there is much to be said for, and nothing against, nylon of at least 20lb breaking strain. As the water warms and the size of fly is reduced, so the breaking strain and thickness of the nylon must fall in order that the fly can swim freely. Generally, I would choose 16lb for a fly of hook size 2; 12lb or 14lb for size 6; 10lb or 8lb for sizes 8 and 10. Below that size, using tiny wisps of tube flies or wee doubles, I might make a careful reduction to 6lb nylon. Such choices would be effected, as I have said, largely by the strength of the current and the nature of the stream. Also, I tend to fish slightly lighter nylon when fishing with the slimmer, lighter long-winged designs, tied on a low-water double hook.

As to leader length, for reasons outlined later, I seldom fish with a longer leader than about 6ft in cold-water conditions, when the fly should be fishing deep. When fishing the sub-surface fly, length would be increased to 9ft, and level nylon in both cases.

The main exception to these general rules comes when I am fishing a very light plastic tube into the teeth of a strong breeze, normally off an intermediate line. This is the only time that I can see any need for a tapered leader, which should have an extra thick butt and steep taper. This is a material aid to fly presentation in a stiff breeze, helping to avoid the light fly being blown back against the casting line.

RODS

Rod strength It may seem odd to jump from leader straight to rod, missing out the line. However, there is a very close relation between leader and rod, and then rod to line; far more so than between leader and line. The leader is the weakest link in the chain and it makes good sense to match the power of the rod to the leader strength. This leads to some quite interesting conclusions.

I presume you are fairly familiar with the AFTM system of rating tackle in as much that if you choose an AFTM 10 rod you will know, in general terms, to partner it with an AFTM 10 line. Equally, a number of authorities suggest that it can be used as a guide in deciding what strength of nylon can be used with a given rod. Generally, this is accepted as offering 2lb of leeway below the AFTM

The Tweed in November. Dusk is a productive time of day, whatever the season (Arthur Oglesby)

Two great salmon anglers, Lee Wulff of America and Arthur Oglesby. British fishermen are seeing the merits of single-handed rods, but in longer lengths than the American 'tooth-picks' (Arthur Oglesby)

number of the rod and so, with an AFTM 6 rod, they would advise against using anything less than 4lb nylon, or 6lb nylon with an AFTM 8 rod. All well and good; this would seem to suggest that, with our AFTM 10 double-handed salmon rod, we can safely fish down to 8lb nylon without any worry. Not so, I'm afraid. We can fish with this light nylon, but we must take extra care and avoid using the full power of the rod when playing a fish.

The reasons are not hard to find when one looks closer at the AFTM system. Firstly, it is important to realise that AFTM stands for the Association of Fishing Tackle Manufacturers *of America*, better described as AFTMA. And, in America, if you talk about double-handed rods, you can expect a visit from the men in white coats. Some of them like to think that there is no need for a longer rod than 9ft for salmon fishing, others prefer a 6ft wand. But they don't have to fish long and heavy flies at the open and close of the season on rivers like the Spey, Tweed and Tay. The point is that they based the system on single-handed rods aerialising only 10yd of line, but it is nothing to lift closer to twice that length with a double-handed rod. Rather than face the task of introducing a new system, British tackle manufacturers quietly adopt and adapt the American one, suiting it to their own and the fisherman's needs; but if we stuck to the rules we would have to describe double-handed rods currently rated at, say, AFTM 11 as AFTM 15 or more.

What this means is that, with our powerful double-handed rods, we can only use them to fight a fish at full potential if our leaders have a breaking strain of not less than about 14lb. That is not to say that they cannot be used with leaders of 12lb or 10lb, but the check should be eased on the reel, the fingers should have a lighter touch on the exposed rim and, generally, a little more care and patience must be shown in fighting the fish.

When we get down to a size 8 fly, we could still be fishing this off 10lb nylon on a double-handed rod but, if we take the step down to 8lb, we might prefer to fish with a less powerful one. It is then that I think about the single-handed rod. It does not have to be unnecessarily short, my own choice being 10ft 6in, a length on which I have killed many of my summer sea trout, grilse and salmon. This rod is rated AFTM 8, quite a powerful rod in the single-handed class; however, it is made up on a superb Lamiglas blank, imported from the States and marketed by Tom Saville. It has a fine, medium action, so unlike those rods with all the action in the tip that are likely to rip the fly from its hold if the salmon shows a last surge of power under the rod tip. This class of rod combines the sensitivity and power that allow leaders down to 6lb with the smallest of flies to be fished with confidence.

Rod length I have just mentioned that I prefer a rod of 10ft 6in for single-handed fishing. I hear the arguments for fishing a shorter length, but cannot see the logic in them. I suppose that, if you prefer to deny yourself casting range and fly control, shorter rods are all well and good, and maybe I am nothing more than a traditionalist, even if I do use a single-handed rod. The ultra-short rod has

The 15ft double-handed rod is the standard armament for larger rivers

no place in the tradition of Scottish fishing or in that of the craftsman who chooses his tools to complete a job with the minimum of effort, and to the best of his abilities.

Many fishermen have settled on a length of 15ft for their double-handed rods, and I agree with them. Certainly there are those who prefer a longer rod, up to 17ft or 18ft on a big, wide river such as the Ness, and such rods are a class apart in their power and casting ability. Their problems, I find, arise in the closing moments of a fight with a fish. Some folk feel that the trouble lies with carbon fibre not having something that they call the 'backbone' to kill a fish, but this arises with any long rod. I remember some of the tussles I had to bring a fish ashore when, as a youngster who spent as much time struggling with the forwards of Tweedside rugby clubs as with the salmon of the area, I fished extremely long split-cane rods. You could buy such rods not so long ago, their ferrules whipped with light wire, but you had to be a bit of a fool to fish with

Playing a salmon on a single-handed rod; ideal for light leaders and small flies

them! With carbon fibre, all that has changed. Rod weight has been vastly reduced. Even so, I would not be happy to fish with a rod of greater than 15ft unless I had a ghillie or companion to land my fish for me. The modern 15ft carbon rod in fact will do all that is asked of it, and is the perfect tool for fishing in cold-water conditions and at those times when we choose to fish the larger class of fly in warm water, certainly in medium-sized and larger rivers.

In the case of smaller rivers, to fish with a 15ft rod might be likened to trying to shoot driven game with an 8-bore goose gun. Recently, on a trip when I had only intended to fish the Spey, I bumped into David Parker who invited me over to fish the Upper Findhorn with him. I felt decidedly over-gunned and cramped with the 15ft rod, and wished I had packed something smaller. There is definitely a place for a rod of 13ft on smaller rivers as an intermediate step between the powerful 15ft rod and the light single-handed.

Rod design As a writer and editor of a sporting magazine, I have had the opportunity to fish with a large number of rods and, because I have fished for a number of years, have witnessed the progression from split cane to glass fibre and then to carbon fibre. Contrary to popular belief, my experience does not extend quite as far as to hickory, lancewood and greenheart!

When glass fibre was introduced, we all thought it was marvellous stuff for salmon rods, and it was not until the introduction of carbon fibre that we realised that it was really not that good. So we all changed over to carbon fibre. Incidentally, cane rods and their predecessors became collector's pieces, but whatever happened to the tens of thousands of glass-fibre rods? Have they simply entered an infinite hibernation on coat racks throughout the land, are they being hoarded by some astute investors waiting for the time when they, too, become collector's pieces, or are they simply staking up peas and beans in the gardens and allotments of Merry England?

Well, whatever happened to them, carbon fibre was here to stay. However, we soon realised that one 'black stick' was not necessarily as good as another. It didn't take long to sort out what was quality and what was rubbish, and what was expensive rubbish and what was value for money. I may not be forgiven for saying this, but we have to remember that fishing tackle is part of a multi-billion investment industry and, as in all businesses, certain people are paid to come up with bright new ideas. So, they told us, it suddenly made a difference whether our rod was black or, say, red; rather like suggesting a car goes faster because it has red stripes painted on its sides or check covers on its seats.

There was one firm, however, Bruce & Walker, who concentrated purely on the quality of its carbon-fibre blanks. The design and action of their rods was hard to beat. The company had been the first to market and manufacture British made fibre-glass rods, and it was Jim Bruce and Ken Walker who manufactured the first British prototype carbon-fibre rod back in the mid-sixties. By the late seventies, they were firmly established in the lead. For quite a few years, many fishermen would have laughed at you if you had suggested that there was a

Ken Walker, of Bruce and Walker Ltd, plays a fish on one of his own rods

better double-handed rod than the Walker 15ft, and simply smiled if you had told them that it could be improved upon. But, there were a lot of serious looking faces when, after much research and development, the company launched their Hexagraph rods onto the fishing scene.

Returning to the 'thrupenny-bit' type profile of the old split-cane rods may have seemed, at first, to be nothing more than some sort of marketing gimmick. It was not. Bruce & Walker produced their own leaflet giving full details of the technical merits of this design. But, accepting that there are inherent problems of ovality in any tubular design, what are the practical benefits of a solid, carbon-strip assembly? Let me emphasise that point. The Hexagraph is not simply another version of the tubular design; it is made from flat carbon strips laid on top of a central, core material. The core material prevents the tendency to flatten and the hexagon shape ensures that a far greater proportion of the fibres are involved in the storage of energy which is instantly released as the rod straightens during the cast. In layman's terms, this creates a more powerful rod. And not only a more powerful casting tool but one which will handle a fish without compromise. Other advantages are increased accuracy and ease of line shooting, although these might be more important in terms of trout rods.

It says a lot about Bruce & Walker's commitment to design that they produce a full range of rods in the 15ft length, from the heavy duty Hexagraph Walker for use with the heaviest of sunk-line tackle through to the Hexagraph Bruce which, while it will certainly handle traditional sunk line, is probably best seen in floating-line fishing.

Personally, because I turn to the single-handed rod for much of my summer salmon fishing, and because I like a powerful rod, I settled on the Hexagraph Walker, AFTM 10–12. If I was utterly committed to the double-handed rod, I might also look at the Hexagraph Bruce rods of 12ft and 13ft, rated for use with lines as light as AFTM 7, and therefore suitable for use with the very lightest of salmon leaders. However, I am only suggesting that you might like to think about these rods. If you have a perfectly good Walker 15ft, there is no point in retiring it and rushing off to replace it with a Hexagraph.

LINES AND BACKING

Fly lines are divided into two main categories: sinking or floating. There is little to be said about floating lines, but sinkers are offered in a large variety from the slowest sinkers of all, known as intermediates or neutral densities, to the extremely fast sinking and sometimes lead-cored lines. In between there are slow, medium, fast, very fast and ultra-fast options. And another class of line must be mentioned, the sink tip – a floating line for all but the last few yards of its length.

I myself use Masterline lines with my double-handed rod. They have a hard, smooth surface and long tapers to aid presentation. Above all, what I like about them, when considering big river fishing, is their 32m length, rather than the standard length of 25m. With the shorter line, when Spey casting with a sympathetic wind it isn't very difficult to put out the full 25m length and, because the tapered section of the line must be within the tip ring if the Spey cast is to be carried out efficiently, I find I am for ever pulling in backing and line preparatory to each cast. With the longer line, there is normally a turn or two of the main line on the reel and whatever handlining I do is far more concerned with fishing technique than ease of casting. However, such a length of line is hardly required on smaller rivers, and certainly not on the single-handed rod.

With the single-handed rod, rated AFTM 8, I use an AFTM 6 Aircel Ultra floating line or, just occasionally, an intermediate. That's another thing about the AFTM system: as we increase the length of line aerialised we increase the load on the rod, so a longer length of AFTM 6 line can be aerialised than of AFTM 8. As I like to fish with about 20yd of line and to reduce handlining, false casting and shooting to a minimum, I favour the lighter line.

As to the various sinking rates of all but the floating line, these should be considered in conjunction with fly weight when we decide upon the depth at which we want to fish, taking into account the nature and strength of the current. As you will have probably realised, in cold-water conditions I tend to prefer a lighter fly than the majority of fishermen because I believe it is more lively and attractive. I like to think of the fly as fishing slightly above or at the same level as the line. Brass tubes, except in the case of the Collie Dog fly, will normally fish below the level of the line, which is why I seldom use them. In a heavy push of water, and where I wish to get my fly down in the depths, I often find myself fishing with an ultra-fast sinker. For more general sunk-line work, I choose a medium sinker.

The intermediate line is used for fishing very light flies just below the surface and, from time to time, in very strong streams, I substitute a medium sinker for this type of work. The sink-tip line, although enormously popular with many fishermen, seldom gets a wetting on my rod. It is held in reserve for those few occasions when I fish a fly at depth to a position well out in the river and where, unless the line can be mended, the fly will be fishing across too quickly.

Having said all this, I am left with the nagging doubt that, simply because I have a full range of six lines from floater to ultra-fast sinking, I put the cart before the horse and seek reasons to justify them all. If limited to just two lines, I don't imagine it would significantly change the number of fish I bring to the bank. Indeed, I fished for many seasons with just two lines – a floater and a fast sinker, the Wetcel 2. If I reverted to that simpler choice of fly line, there would certainly be times when I would wonder whether an intermediate might not present the warm-water flies that little bit more attractively, but such a line is not nearly as pleasant to cast and control as the floater. Also, the depth at which a line fishes is not simply a matter of its sinking rate. The slower it fishes, the deeper it goes, as I hope to show in the chapter on casting and presentation.

A further division in salmon lines is whether they are double-taper or weight-forward, in which I include shooting heads. The choice lies largely with the method of casting employed. The weight-forward is an excellent choice for overhead casting, but it is not at all easy to mend with such a line. The double-taper is perfectly adequate for overhead casting, and offers more delicate presentation and far easier control. In Spey casting, something that I do whether I am fishing a floater or a sinker on the double-handed rod, the double-taper is essential; which is why I avoid the weight-forward line for all normal fishing situations.

The line should be of the right weight to balance the power of the rod. It must be heavy enough to work the rod properly and bring out its action, but not so heavy as to strain it. With single-handed rods, the problem is far simpler, but with double-handed rods it may be worth experimenting in order to discover which weight of line suits a particular rod best. Some say that rod manufacturers are too careful of their rods, and do not wish them to be strained; others argue that they overline their rods to ensure the action is brought out with far too short a length of line! Personal preference, as well as the individual's normal length of line, play their part. With my current Walker Hexagraph 15ft, rated at AFTM 10–12, I like an 11 line; but some prefer to go up or down a weight.

Behind the main casting line, there is the backing. I prefer to use monofilament nylon of about 25lb breaking strain because, firstly it does not rot; secondly it doesn't take up too much room allowing plenty of length to be put on the reel and, lastly, it is relatively cheap.

On small rivers, the backing may seldom be called into play but, on a medium-sized river, it is certainly advisable to have close to 100yd in reserve. You never know when you might need it if a fish of a lifetime sets off in a heavy stream. I remember a fish that I hooked in the tail race from the aluminium smelting works on the Lochy. That fish used the stream to accelerate its progress straight back to the sea. It was like a scene from a Hemingway story of marlin fishing as the backing tore off and the reel screamed. On big rivers, many fishermen would consider 125yd a safer margin, and it is always better to be cautious.

Much of the strength of nylon lies in its elasticity. It is stretched when a large fish plays hard. Therefore, depending on where and how often the backing is called into play, it should be renewed at fairly regular intervals and it should certainly be checked from end to end quite frequently.

REELS

There are a number of good reels offered for use with double-handed rods. At the bottom end of the scale, in terms of price, are reels such as the Leeda Rimfly Magnum, a smallish reel but quite suitable for somebody who doesn't want to spend too much money and is not planning to fish the bigger rivers where a good length of backing is required. Even at this end of the market, the reel is fitted with an adjustable check, exposed rim and optional left- or right-hand wind. Toward the upper end of the scale are the Hardy Marquis reels. The Hardy name is traditionally synonymous with quality and their reels are fine pieces of engineering. They are very fine fishing tools for those prepared to spend a few pounds more. In the middle of the range are perfectly satisfactory and functional reels such as those offered by Bruce & Walker and the Shakespeare Beaulite, which is a reel I have used since my student days.

If I have a criticism to make of modern salmon reels, it is that they have not kept up with the advances in other tackle. Carbon rods turned out to be marvellous casting tools and, certainly for Spey casting, led to a demand for longer fly lines which are produced in up to 40yd lengths. Equally, many fishermen prefer to fish with heavy lines, AFTM 11 or 12, but have you seen how quickly the bulk of 40yd of AFTM 12 floating line fills a spool? There is not much space left for the essential length of backing associated with big, wide rivers which, after all, are the places where such line is likely to be used. I, for one, would like to see some slightly larger reels, in terms of diameter rather than the width of the spool.

The weight of line must balance the power of the rod

Modern reels of functional design

For my single-handed rod, I use a Leeda Dragonfly reel. These are relatively inexpensive, but are the first and only item of fishing tackle ever to receive a Design Award. With exposed rim and variable check, essential in any salmon reel, their lightweight carbon construction is perfectly suited to the modern generation of lightweight carbon rods. Either the Kingsize 100 or the Imperial 120, which holds 100yd of backing behind an AFTM 9 line, is my first choice.

WADERS

Armed with flies, leaders, lines, reel and rod, the fisherman can approach a river and catch a salmon. These five items are the fisherman's fixed assets. The only other item that comes close to being included in the essential category is a good pair of waders. It is possible to fish smaller rivers in thigh waders, some can be adequately covered in Wellingtons and others require climbing boots; but the salmon fisherman is best advised to think in terms of chest waders. On medium-sized rivers, they may seldom be used to their full potential, but it is comforting to know that the extra free-board is there if required.

Chest waders can be purchased complete with boots attached or as stockings to be used with separate brogues. I have both types. The separate brogue certainly provides the more substantial alternative, providing much greater protection and support for the ankles when the going gets tough, but is not as easy to slip on and off. The most important consideration, other than the uppers' ability to take a fair bit of wear and tear, is the foothold. Plain, rubber soles are the equivalent of suicide in a rocky river. Metal studs are far better; felt soles with studded heels are better still.

Safety in wading is an important consideration. It is not simply a matter of choosing the best grip for the sole of the boot. Even with the best grips, there is an ever present risk of a ducking, particularly on the larger, more powerful rivers such as the Spey. A ducking need not be fatal, but it is always unpleasant and, besides anything else, a waste of good fishing time. The true professional in a dangerous situation, whether he be soldier or stuntman, decides what is an acceptable level of risk. Confidence and ability in deep wading are essential qualifications in certain situations, but that should never make us reckless. It is said in shooting that 'all the pheasants ever bred, won't repay for one man dead', and widows and orphans will be singularly unimpressed with the explanation that he was tempted out onto that long hog-back of gravel leading into deep swirling water by the sight of a head-and-tailing grilse. Lest I am accused of being sexist, in refering to widow rather than widower, I hasten to say that the female of the species usually has more sense.

Deep wading is an integral part of fly fishing on larger rivers

On the subject of danger, it seems a great pity that more ghillies, when dealing with an obviously inexperienced or elderly fisherman, or one new to the beat, do not see their duties as extending beyond advice on choice of fly and which pool to try it in before settling comfortably, net at hand, to watch the world pass by rather than donning a pair of waders and accompanying the angler. On too many occasions when finding myself in a tricky place or finding a pot-hole the hard way, my muttered comments to the stony-faced figure relaxing on the shore have been lost in the rushing of the stream.

There are a few basic rules of wading which should be observed. Never step onto a large rock; go round it. Treat shingle-bottomed pools with the greatest of respect, often the stream is fast and the bottom shelves into deeper water; it is not funny to be standing on top of a miniature landslide carrying you into deep water and the prospect of hundreds of yards of open pool below you. Never try to turn round in a strong stream; shuffle backwards. Be aware of your buoyancy in deep water. I have an ample girth-to-length ratio coupled to a low centre of gravity, but I am very familiar with the 'bounce'. However much weight you may be applying per square inch of boot sole, there comes a point when you may, quite literally, float away, or at least have insufficient weight, due to buoyancy, to get a secure anchor in a heavy push of water – again, away you go.

The bounce can also be used to the advantage of a deep wader in difficulties. Aiming yourself inshore, with head back to raise the level of nose and mouth, go downstream as fast as you can in a series of vertical bounces along the river bed. You may start shipping some water, but do not worry, you will have another foot of depth before the water comes over your face. Of course, you can look fairly silly if you are running straight into deeper water, but I have got myself out of awkward situations before by this method and would not hesitate to use it again. If you must bounce, at least try to do it constructively!

'If it's inevitable, lie back and enjoy it', is a fatuous statement in the context with which it is normally associated. And yet, in salmon fishing, I have seen experienced waders actually laughing at their own mistake as they floated by, heading for shallow water.

There are a couple of popular misconceptions about waders and wading accidents. Firstly, there are people who assert that waders will be full of air when a fisherman falls over. It is suggested that this can be very dangerous because, if all the air rushes to the feet, the fisherman will be upended, with his feet above the water and his head below. This is nonsense. The pressure of the water against the waders forces the air out, just like crushing a bag in your hand, and there is only a small amount of air left, trapped in the clothing. It is just enough to be a small help in keeping the fisherman afloat, but nothing more.

Secondly it is said that if the waders fill with water, the water will, being heavier than air, pull him down. Again, this is nonsense. Certainly, it would be true that if the fisherman's waders had filled with water and he was standing on the river bank they would feel heavy, but we are not talking about water in air, we are talking about water in water, and water in water is no heavier than air in air. It neither floats nor sinks because it has neutral density.

The real danger in wading is panic. Make no mistake, it is panic that kills. The first instinct, whether stepping into an icy wind or cold shower is a sharp intake of breath. The problem is that, in the river, with our heads underwater, we will be shipping a cargo of water rather than air. We cough and splutter, taking in more water and, other than being dragged out and resuscitated, we are in very deep trouble.

When the swimmer dives into cold water, he knows that he cannot breathe until he surfaces; the wader, in the second that he tumbles, must have the same determination. If you have time, take a deep breath before you go under.

If a fisherman finds himself actually underwater, his first concern is to get to the surface. As already mentioned there will be just sufficient air in the lungs and trapped in the clothing, between waders and body, to float him. The arms must be kept firmly at the sides, but a little wrist-flapping and foot-kicking will speed the moment when the head pops through the surface. Float on your back, feet pointing downstream and, again, take a deep breath to improve buoyancy, then breathe as gently as possible to maintain the maximum amount of air in the lungs. Now is the time to survey the bankside scene for a suitable landing place. There is absolutely no point in trying to drag yourself out up a high bank. Aim for an area of shallow shingle. When there, never try to stand up immediately; get yourself out of the river on all fours. You will be weak from your exertions, the water in your waders will be heavy now that you are in the air, and there is every possibility that you will fall over and injure yourself.

When you've got your breath back, get straight to your car, strip, towel yourself down, get into dry clothes and have a cup of hot coffee or tea. No, do not have a dram; not now anyway. It simply speeds up the heat loss from your body. Gin is the perfect excuse for keeping you cool in the tropics, but the glow induced by a dram in cold weather is a transient thing and, in this situation, to be strongly avoided. Right, now that you're feeling better, get into your spare waders and back into the river.

So there we have a few items of near essential equipment: a towel, a change of clothes, a flask of hot coffee or similar, a spare pair of waders if you can possibly afford them and, finally, considering the combination of a strong fright with cold water, a pack of tissues or a roll of loo paper.

BITS AND PIECES

There are many items of tackle which, whilst not absolutely essential, are very useful.

Scissors of the folding variety, where the points are sheathed into the handles, are perfectly safe and ready to hand when carried on a loop around the neck. A thermometer gives interesting and very useful information on both air and water temperatures. This has a very important bearing in deciding suitable tackle and techniques. The pen variety is sturdy, and can be safely carried in a pocket.

Adhesive tape, otherwise known as insulating tape and available from hardware shops, has a multiplicity of uses in making running repairs. And, until the rod manufacturers come up with a better way of jointing their rods, it will be essential to continue to ensure that the rod does not fly apart when casting by taping up the joints. Even in the modern age of high-tech we have to resort to little bits of sticky tape to hold our space-age material rods together and, with certain manufacturers' rods, it is even necessary to tape the reel in place!

What else would be useful? A stub of candle to wax the rod ferrules of carbon and fibre-glass rods; a slip of stone to sharpen hooks; a spare spring for the reel which, while seldom needed, can avoid ruination of a day's fishing; a wader repair kit which can save a lot of discomfort.

5

FLY CASTING AND PRESENTATION

In the last chapter I outlined the tackle involved in fishing the fly. I said that, like the good workman, who never blames his tools, we should ensure that our tackle is beyond reproach. Other than in exceptional circumstances, totally inadequate tackle is unlikely. What is far more likely is that the fisherman may not have the skill and ability to use his tackle to its full potential.

Particularly in terms of the largest rivers such as the Ness, Spey and Tay, the ability to cast a long line and wade deep is absolutely vital to success. True, you have to know something of the general behaviour pattern of the fish and what fly is most likely to stimulate the desired taking response but, if you cannot cast far enough to show the fly to the salmon, all the knowledge in the world will be totally useless.

And it is not simply a case of showing the fly to the salmon in any old fashion. The fly must be presented correctly which, in most cases, means as slowly as possible. There are times, of course, when we cast quite squarely, even upstream, but these are tactics associated with specialised situations in low, warm water. Modern fly fishing for salmon, in general terms, depends very heavily on casting a long line downstream at a relatively shallow angle.

One day, when fishing the middle Spey, I stopped for a chat with the ghillie. As we talked, I caught sight of a fish, just a quick head and tail roll, far out in a very powerful stream. The ghillie said that there was a great slab of rock between the two mainstreams where running fish tended to pause, but not for long. He warned me that it involved a nasty wade and some long casting to cover the fish, and insisted that I should take a wading staff.

Have you ever felt the full weight of the Spey in its faster sections as it seeks to sweep you away to Speymouth? And when the river bed is a heaving mass of football-sized and larger boulders, believe me, it can be a hair-raising experience. Eventually I shuffled into position, way out in the river but inshore, and some 25yd upstream of where the fish had been showing. I lengthened line and began casting, picturing the long-winged Munro Killer, tied on a size 4 low-water double hook, hovering slowly across the strong stream. I lost count of the number of casts that I made. By now I was throwing as large a mend as I could manage, shooting hand-held line in the process; quite literally dangling the fly over the fish's nose. Then slowly, oh so slowly, the line tightened; the reel clicked once, twice, accelerating into song before I clamped the line with my hand and

It takes skill and ability to use tackle to its full potential

raised the rod tip. Ignoring the fish, I put the rod over my shoulder, and set out on the torturous wade back to the shore.

I can't remember another time when dry land felt so good under my feet. The subsequent tussle and eventual netting of the fish, however, were nothing compared to that brief moment of satisfaction when a combination of deep wading, long casting and line control had produced the thrilling message of a taking fish. The cast is the basis of it all.

OVERHEAD AND SPEY CASTING

The overhead is the basic 'tick-tock' cast that we all start by learning, particularly if we come to salmon fishing after serving our apprenticeship with trout. It is normally quite adequate for those who fish smaller rivers and, there is no denying, skilled practitioners can put out a good length of line when faced with larger waters. However, because the line is carried back behind the fisherman, it cannot be used where trees or a high bank are immediately behind the caster. There is also the ever present risk of wind knots forming in the leader and weakening it and, when a long line is being used, there is a risk that the fly may touch on a stone during the back cast. The point can then be broken and, if a fish takes, the fisherman will have nothing but the depth of his vocabulary to comfort him.

Although a good practitioner can put out a good length of line with an overhead cast, with the Spey cast he can achieve far greater distances with less effort. The late John Ashley Cooper stated that 35yd is none too long a distance to aim at when fishing the larger rivers. Try doing that with an overhead, not once or twice but throughout the whole of a long fishing day! Although we may not be able to reach the prodigious lengths of the maestros, consistent long casting is far easier with the Spey, either single or double.

There seem, however, to be two schools of thought on Spey casting. Those who can do it sing its praises; those who can't, criticise it. Yet once a fisherman has learnt to Spey cast, and realises the enormous advantages, he is loathe to use any other method. It is perhaps unfortunate that something of a mystique has grown up around it. It is relatively easy to describe the overhead cast and produce diagrams because it is very largely a two-dimensional, back and forth, type of cast. To describe the single Spey cast can end in utter confusion, but it is

Casting practise on a fishing course

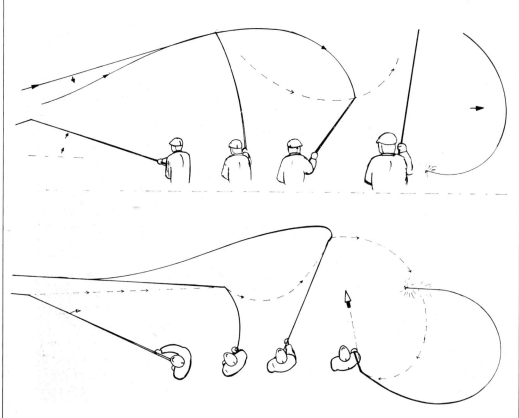

The single Spey cast. Confused? It's hardly surprising: the only way to learn this cast is from practical instruction and then practise, practise, practise!

really very easy. I have been shown it by many folk, from ghillies who have used it all their lives to some of this country's most noted writers and professional instructors. They all have their little niceties of style, but it is the Speyside ghillie who makes the least fuss about the whole thing. Arthur Oglesby casts in a very similar style, only he is three times better than most at explaining it, and ten times better at spotting and correcting faults in others. Such an instructor can work miracles on the most raw of novices in a very short time.

I have tried on a number of occasions to put down in print the technique of the single and double Spey casts. All descriptions over-complicate what is, at its most basic, a very simple set of actions. The single Spey is little more than a pointing of the rod down the line, a raising of the rod near to the vertical, a U-shaped swing and a final chuck of the line. Either can be demonstrated and shown in a few minutes on the river bank. After that, all that is needed is long hours of practice in order to perfect the timing of the cast. I have learnt a lot by simply taking time off to watch skilled local fishermen making the Spey cast look easy. And don't make the mistake of thinking that, just because of the name, the

Once learnt, the double Spey cast is relatively simple, very safe and highly effective

double Spey is harder. More than one novice has turned to me with a smile and said, 'But I though it would be more difficult than that.' It is only difficult to do it really well. Other than that the double Spey is undoubtedly one of the safest of casts and the one I normally use, following a roll cast to clear the line from the water, when fishing a sunken line.

PRESENTATION

In discussing the taking behaviour of fish and the stimulus that was likely to tip the scales from the normal, non-taking behaviour pattern to disinhibition, I said that the movement of the fly, the way it swims, is every bit as important as its physical appearance. We can affect the fly's behaviour by varying its design. For example, as we have seen, the lighter we make a fly in proportion to its total surface area, the more lively it will be, responding to the vagaries of the stream, darting here, hovering there. But that is not the end of the story. We can radically affect the behaviour of the fly by controlling its water speed. This, very largely, is achieved by alterations in the angle of presentation.

A previous generation of fishermen, influenced very heavily by the pronounce-ments of Arthur Wood and his disciples who employed the classic 'greased line' method of fishing, believed they were fishing with, and catching salmon on, a fly that fished in the stream like a drifting leaf, entirely without drag. Ignoring the fact that they were simply fooling themselves in believing that their flies could fish in such a way, nowadays we accept that a salmon is not really likely to show any interest in something that appears dead in the water. Even in fishing the dry fly, a little drag seems to improve the presentation, certainly in these islands.

It seems that it is some sort of lifelike motion in the swimming salmon fly that provokes a response, and this is solely what the majority of fishermen seem to provide. They cast out their flies diagonally across the stream, never varying the angle of presentation, irrespective of the speed of the current, and seem to forget about how the fly is behaving until it is time to cast again. They leave it all to the current, and take no active part in effecting how the fly swims. With the fly hanging in the stream below them, they draw in a couple of yards of line, take a couple of paces, cast, and so the process is repeated down the length of that pool and the next one, and the next one.

Why is that? Well, I suspect it is because so often in salmon fishing there is an awful long time between one fish and the next. The mind does tend to wander. How often, when fishing a long salmon pool, do we find our mind is anywhere but on the job in hand. Then a fish shows in that lazy, tantalising porpoise roll and our adrenalin starts to flow. We concentrate hard and, for a few minutes, we are fishing at full potential. But maintaining that concentration for long periods when we are not making any contact is desperately hard. That is why, as I have suggested elsewhere in this book, there are times to sow and times to reap. There seems little point in fishing so hard through times unlikely to produce a taking fish that, when the magical moment arrives, we are too exhausted and disinterested to make the most of it. Far better to relax through the long heat of a summer's afternoon and arrive fresh and raring to go in the last few hours of daylight than to fish on and, as dusk approaches, find that we can think of little else than the hotel bar, dinner and a comfortable chair in the lounge.

I was speaking recently to a very well-known person who has fished as a guest of a very keen and successful fisherman; a very hard task-master who expects his guests to fish with the same total devotion to the job in hand as himself. At the end of a long, hard day on the river, he told me that he had, quite literally, fallen asleep in midstream, and had only woken when a cold draught of water spilt into his chest waders. How much concentration was he giving to the manner in which his fly was fishing?

If you won't take my word for it that fly control is important, read these words of John Ashley Cooper which appeared in *A Line on Salmon*: '. . . the intelligent fisherman who uses his imagination, and can transmit his will-power to the passage of his fly through the water, as opposed to simply letting the current do it for him (if it will), will catch two or three times as many fish.'

In practically all salmon fishing situations, our control of the fly is concerned primarily with ensuring that it is not swimming unnaturally fast. There are times of course when, even if we hang our fly, it will have an unnaturally high water speed. I am thinking of warm-water conditions, suggesting the use of a relatively small fly, but where fish are lying in or on the cheeks of a strong stream, so strong that no small creature could avoid being swept away in it. At such times, we have to swop our fly for something far larger, say a Collie Dog with 3in or 4in of trailing wing, or a long tube fly, and still fish it as slowly as possible. I wonder how often in the summer months we use flies that are far too small, following blindly the traditional advice on salmon fishing. And then, having decided to use a larger than normal fly, what should we do when it has swung into slacker water? It seems only logical that it must be handlined back, possibly quite quickly, in order to maintain the semblance of life.

Having established that there is a need to control the water speed of the fly, we can look at methods which will help us to achieve it. These break down into two separate categories based on whether they are methods to decrease or increase the water speed of the fly. Let's start by looking at methods that slow down the passage of the fly.

Casting angle When the line is hanging straight downstream from the rod tip, it is stationary, and the fly hovers in the stream. Its water speed is no greater than

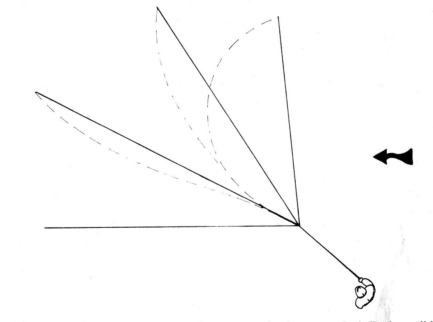

Avoiding belly in the line: the squarer the cast is made, the greater the belly that will be created in the line

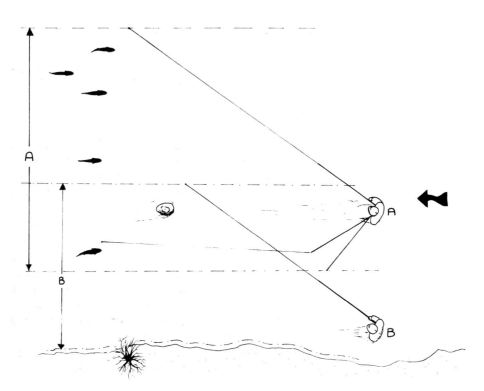

The advantages of long casting and deep wading in terms of water coverage with cast of same angle

that of the current; and this represents the minimum speed at which a fly can be fished, other than casting it upstream and allowing it to drift down, when its water speed is nil, although it may be moving quite quickly in relation to the river bank. If the line is cast straight across the stream, this produces maximum water speed. A belly forms in the line and whips the fly across and down.

We cannot fish the fly at its minimum speed, hanging straight down in the current, by normal fly-fishing methods, because we would be so limited in terms of water coverage. However, what can be achieved by this method can be seen when we harl a fly or spinner over the stern of a boat. Equally, except in exceptional circumstances, we will not wish to fish the fly at its maximum speed, represented by a square cast. Therefore, some sort of a compromise must be reached.

The compromise is that, although it is possible to cast fairly square in the slowest of stretches of water, we must reduce our casting angle as the speed of the stream increases. Thus, we would start in the fast neck of a pool by casting at a relatively shallow angle, gradually widening the angle as we fish through the slower body of the pool, then getting ever shallower as we move back into faster water accelerating toward the glide and tail of the pool.

As the casting angle is reduced, so the ability to cast a long line and wade deep becomes so much more important if we are to achieve adequate water coverage and not simply fish a very narrow strip of water, close inshore. And, without those abilities, the temptation is always there to cast at too wide an angle, thus covering the fish, but ineffectively.

Mending the line   This method of controlling the water speed of the fly was popularised by Arthur Wood of greased-line fame. It is certainly most easily achieved with a floating line although it is possible, if not necessarily easy, to throw in one good mend before a sinking line has gone below the surface. Mending the sinking line is dealt with in greater detail in Chapter 6.

An upstream mend is what is required to slow down the passage of the fly. You know that a downstream belly in the line will pull the fly across the stream and it is by reversing this, by throwing an upstream belly into the line, that we are able to reduce the water speed of the fly. A mend is carried out by pointing the rod down the line and pushing the point of the rod through an oval, lifting the line from the water and switching it into an upstream loop. In practice, this is not a difficult manoeuvre but it takes a certain nicety of touch to ensure that only the line is moved, and not the leader and fly. It needs a smooth motion, without any trace of jerkiness. Like the Spey cast it is hard to describe in words, easy to demonstrate, and learnt through practice, practice and more practice.

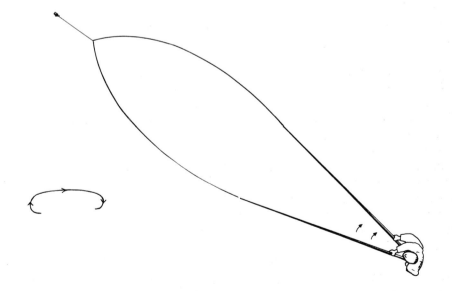

Mending is used to place an upstream or downstream belly in the line, to speed up or slow down the passage of the fly. In making a mend, the leader and fly should not move. Rod tip follows this line

6

COLD-WATER TACTICS

Soaking in a hot bath with only a dram for company, I have taken stock and wondered whether it is all worthwhile. In the cold, searing wind of morning, I shall be back at the river. The water's icy grip will penetrate waders and thick layers of clothing until, finally, it stabs to the bone. Nobody but a fellow fisherman could appreciate that there is any enjoyment in fishing the opening days of the season. I begin to doubt it myself. But when the line draws away, tightening in the depths of the dark, mysterious pool, when yards of line are stripped from the reel as the first springer of the season raises a shower of spray, I will have no more doubts.

Water temperatures remain below 50°F for a great part of the British salmon season. That is why the range of our tactics and thinking on salmon are so much broader than those of the Americans. They have their main runs in the summer months. That is why they think in terms of single-handed rods. What can they know of the gale-torn glens and straths, of days when the ice has to be broken and floated away before fishing can be started? Take them to the Helmsdale or Oykel, Spey or Dee at the opening of the season, to the Tay or Tweed at its close; then they will know something of our rivers and our salmon.

Cold-water techniques hold a deep fascination for me. Those who limit their salmon-fishing experience to the summer months, the holiday fishermen, have no need for them. But the ability to make the most of powerful tackle with deep and slow tactics is essential to those who pursue salmon throughout the long season, from as early as January until the very end of November.

It is not simply the techniques of cold-water fly fishing that are so challenging and fascinating. There are the fish that we hope to encounter. Few fish are so highly prized as the fresh-run springer with its deep, silvery flank, as hard in the flesh as a prize-fighter. It throws down a challenge that leads us on long and hazardous winter journeys into a harsh environment. There are no questions as to the value of the springer.

Autumn fish, on the other hand, come in for a high degree of discussion and criticism. Some folk try to make them the scapegoat for diminished spring runs, arguing that late-running fish disturb and destroy the eggs of earlier spawning fish. But we know from history that there have been other times when the autumn fish dominated our salmon stocks. Why, then, did the spring fish not die out hundreds of years ago?

Cold and hard work. The glasses are to protect the eyes from the possibility of a mis-timed cast, rather than due to a hint of sunshine

It is impossible to say when the autumn run stops to make way for the springers. Tweed, in late November, can produce mixed bags of late-running autumn fish and the earliest of the springers, though these fish may have entered the river on the same day. Salmon run suitable rivers throughout the winter months, and it is these winter fish that can produce brisk sport on rivers such as the Tay and Tweed from the opening day of the season. Would it take much of a nudge from nature, some shift in the polar ice-cap or drift in the ocean currents, for the bulk of late-running autumn fish to alter their character, delay their arrival by a few weeks, and return us to an age of great spring fishings?

Tweed appears to operate on a thirty-year cycle between its heaviest runs occurring in spring or autumn. Of one thing I am sure: if man chooses to intervene in such matters, making some conceited attempt to manipulate salmon runs, he is more than just likely to make a mess of it.

Some people say that autumn fish are so close to spawning that we should stop all fishing and offer the salmon free passage to the redds. They talk of gravid fish in their tartan breeks and unfit to eat. What they fail to recognise is the difference between taking fish in autumn, and the taking of autumn fish.

Certainly there is no excuse for killing fish that entered the river in spring and summer, and have become stale and potted. There is probably little harm in taking the odd stale cock fish for smoking, but what sort of mentality kills the heavily pregnant female of any species? In purely logical terms, there may seem to be no difference between killing a hen fish in June as she enters the river, or in October as she nears the redds. Either way, it is one less belly full of spawn to continue the species. So, it is purely a moral argument, but no gravid hen fish shall die at my hand.

Clean, fresh-run autumn fish, pouring in from the sea at the back-end of the season, are an entirely different matter. Here are fish worthy of any sportsman's attention. I live on the Solway where we enjoy tremendous runs of autumn salmon. We may bemoan the lack of spring fish but, without our autumn fish, such rivers as the Annan, Border Esk, Nith and other lesser known waters would be notable only for their sea trout. The harvest runs to many thousands of fish, but these are autumn-running fish that we catch and this, as I have said, is a very different matter from killing fish in autumn!

As on the Nith on the western side of Scotland, so on Tweedside is the salmon season extended to the end of November, and fish are running clean and strong at that date. Salmon in their tens of thousands run fast and hard off the tide and on to the upstream beats. Given the right conditions, they can offer a splendid bonanza of sport.

THE RIGHT CONDITIONS

I have just said 'given the right conditions', and what tales of sorrow and frustration lie behind those words. The opening months of the season can see rivers iced over from bank to bank or, far worse, that damnable suspension of ice crystals, known as 'grue', filling the river. Ice can be broken, but until grue clears you might as well fish in a bucket. And again, at the close of the season, we are often faced with high, cold floods. We can pray for an overnight frost at such times on Tweed; it will close the tap on the run-off from bankside fields, the ruinous flow from forestry drains and road washings. We look to the river to drop several feet but still run high and, above all, for the water to clear. Now we start to fish with confidence.

Tweed and other lowland rivers running through rich, agricultural land in their lower reaches and extensive forestry plantings with their associated drainage schemes on the headwaters, can run the colour of potter's clay in a spate. They fill with sticks and debris or the bloated carcase of a dead ewe and, if it is autumn, the fisherman will have to contend with a snowstorm of fallen leaves filling the river. Lowland waters become unfishable in a pea souper of a spate.

Highland rivers, some of them at least, can give the appearance of being fishable almost immediatley after the height of a spate, but they are not. They suffer from what we call 'black' spates, and simply because they do not run the

At the start of the season, water levels will normally be high

colour of mud does not imply that fish can be caught. The flotsam and jetsam of a spate on such rivers acts as a pointer to the fishing conditions. As the debris and froth clear, so the fishing improves.

Of course, at any time of the season, be it spring or autumn, probably better described as late or early winter, we may be faced with low water. But for most of the time from January until May, and again from September to the close of the season, water levels will normally be high.

FISH BEHAVIOUR

Time of year has a strong effect on the salmon's reaction to high water. At the very start of the season and until temperatures struggle up and away from freezing point, salmon may do little more than nose their way into the lower pools. Fish, as we have seen, are reluctant to enter rivers until their temperature exceeds that of the sea. In the lowest temperatures, during a spate, spring salmon will stop running and bide where they are until the river has fallen back to near its normal level. They will stop at any obstacle that hinders their free passage. At the start of the Tweed season, salmon will be found in deep water at the edge of the main streams and in the deep dubs, but it would be rare for fresh fish to penetrate further upstream than the junction with the Teviot.

As the season progresses into rather warmer conditions, fish seem more ready to adopt lies in streamier water. It can be surprising to discover the strength of current in which a salmon seems prepared to rest, albeit sometimes briefly. It is exciting work to fish a big fly during a late-spring spate. We might be fishing a long and provocative Collie Dog with 6in or more of hair-wing to shimmer and shimmy across the fish's view. Such a fly can produce very positive takes. Or it might be a long, Brora-style, wire-bodied fly that is doing the business.

If the salmon of the start of the season are characterised by slow running behaviour, it is probably because there is little need for them to behave otherwise. Late season fish, on the other hand, are like businessmen who find themselves already late for an important appointment. There is much more hustle and bustle about the salmon of autumn.

Many experienced fishermen will tell you that spring salmon are not difficult to tempt, only to find. It certainly seems that a proportion of them run the river in batches and it may come down to a little judgement and a lot of luck in being at the right pool at the right time as a small group fans up from the tail in search of temporary resting places. The fisherman who arrives at the pool an hour or so later may find that batch has moved on.

In high water, I would be expecting salmon in deepish areas of water with a jumble of rocks and boulders strewn close into the bank, and definitely on the inside curve of the river to provide shelter from the main force of the current. The river bank offers clear evidence as to what is happening on the river bed. If the bank is strewn with rocks, it is a fairly safe bet that the bed will be the same. Similarly, a steep bank points to deep water close in, whereas a shelving bank is associated with an area of shallows.

Over these rocky areas the surface may be turbulent, but I picture the salmon lying in the small pockets of shelter created by the boulders. Salmon seem to like

Lessons from the river bank: a gentle slope indicates a shallow area. A steep bank and rocks will carry down to the river bed

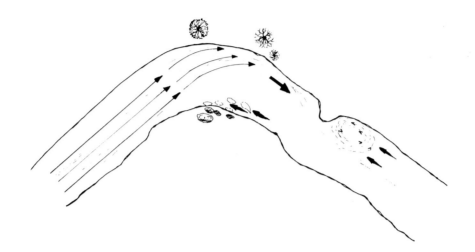

Two favourite resting places in high water: in a jumble of rocks on an inside curve, and just below a back-water

nothing better than to fin gently in a nook of comfort surrounded by faster water, with their bellies resting on a slab of rock. I believe that a certain pattern of flow will hold a salmon down onto a rock, and experienced salmon fishermen are familiar with the abrasions on a salmon's belly and chin that we associate with high water.

To say that salmon will lie in backwaters during high water is no more than a half-truth. My experience is that salmon will not lie actually in the area of contra flow. They will, however, take up station just downstream of such an area, where the current gathers momentum back into the main stream. Such a spot is not easily fished. You cast out over the backwater and your line comes snaking back upstream toward where you are standing on the bank. Such areas are probably best fished from a boat or from the opposite bank if possible.

I once drove five miles up a glen, to cross at the bridge, and then the five miles back down the opposite bank of the high and unwadable river, just to fish such a lie. With a long cast and an enormous upstream mend thrown in just before the line sank, I hoped that the fly would be fishing across the lie attractively. I was edging further out across the stream with every cast, and feeling a little wary at the push of the stream on my back, when the reel clicked hesitantly before accelerating into a long song of whirring reel handle. As it slowed, I tightened into a hard tussle with a beautifully fresh fish, straight off the tide. Shortly afterwards, from the same draw, I hooked the twin of the first fish. The drive seemed far more than simply worthwhile.

Sooner or later, water levels will fall away. The more normal lies along the cheeks of the mainstreams will be able to provide adequate shelter once again, and we shall return to fishing the pools rather than clearly defined and localised holding spots.

TACKLE AND TECHNIQUES

The techniques of cold-water fly fishing is traditionally described as 'deep and slow'. It may seem to be splitting hairs, but in many ways it would be more accurate to say 'close to the fish and at a natural speed'. However, before looking at that a little more closely, let's consider tackle.

The choice of sound and adequate tackle is basic to success in salmon fishing, and never more so than when we are fishing with sinking lines. As we shall see, cold-water fly fishing places great strains on tackle. It takes a powerful rod to fish a long length of sinking line effectively. Such a rod must have the action and length to roll and double Spey a fast sinker, and it is easy to snap a weak rod.

Most fishermen use tube flies, on brass or aluminium bodies, but I prefer the wire-bodied, Brora style of fly which casts, fishes and hooks so effectively. I have seen tube flies where, after a hard day's fishing, the nylon leader has cut through the inner plastic core, and I fret that the leader may cut on the metal when I am playing a fish. But tens of thousands of salmon have been taken on metal tube flies so, if you like them, use them.

I like the long, slim profile of these articulated flies. Many of them tend to be rather overdressed, and I always make a point, in tying my own, of ensuring that the wing is kept in proportion. As to colour, black, yellow and orange create a most successful wing for a long salmon fly, and I normally fish a Willie Gunn type, increasing the proportions of yellow and orange for use in coloured water, and of the black when the water has cleared. Do such things make any difference

Light v heavy: a light fly fished above a fast sinking line swims attractively; far more so than a heavy fly below a slower sinker

to the salmon? I suspect they do, and therefore it gives me greater confidence to reduce or increase the visibility of the fly.

Fairly light bodies to the flies are my preference. Light flies, to my mind, create a far more deadly stimulus than the alternative heavy, dull and lifeless ones, fished off a slow sinker or, as I have seen on the Spey, a full floater. The latter undoubtedly makes for easy casting, but I do not see how a super-heavy fly hanging below a floater can fish effectively. The faster sinking line with a light fly, to fish at the same depth as a slow sinker and heavy fly, is the more difficult casting tool. That is why I use a short leader. Having gone to the bother of casting and presenting a fast sinking line, I don't want my light fly to be fishing too far above it, so I only give it about 6ft of nylon, seldom more, on which to play.

This statement that the faster sinking line is a less pleasant line to cast than a slower sinker, needs some qualification. The weight of a very heavy fly on the slower line can lead to all sorts of problems in casting, and requires an alteration in casting technique; it might be likened to a heavy stone on a piece of string. If the heavy fly appeals to you, there is one little piece of advice: be sure to use a strong leader, a minimum of 25lb nylon. That heavy fly is going to be moving like a bullet if you choose to overhead cast and, while my own view is that super-heavy flies are better thrown away, you might not agree when such a fly snaps your leader as if it were sewing cotton.

Fishing the fly Deep and slow, as I have said, are the watch-words of the early and late season salmon fisherman, but this begs the question 'how deep and how slow?' To a certain extent, the answer differs according to the river being fished.

Depth of fly: it is better to think in terms of height above fish rather than depth below surface. In cold water conditions, the fly should be quite close to the fish

The late Reg Righyni fishing a Tweed pool

Depth is a fascinating fishing concept. I hope I shall be excused for suggesting that the majority of anglers stand it on its head. They talk about depth below the surface, which might be right for warm-water fishing but, in cold water, what we should be talking about is depth, or rather height, above the river bed. Salmon lie in all sorts of depth of water. As the water warms into the forties, many of them are to be found lying at the cheeks of streams as they spread into the body of the pool, in water of about 4ft to 6ft in depth.

Salmon are lethargic in cold water, compared to their warm-water behaviour, but they are still streamlined, predatory torpedoes. There is no need to treat them like zombies and imagine that our fly must bump them on the nose if they are to take any notice of it. But, to be on the safe side, it is best to fish the fly within a foot or two of them. And that means, in water of about 5ft, that our fly should be fishing at 2ft to 3ft below the surface.

This might be considered fairly typical of much of the fishing on relatively shallow rivers such as the Spey, but what about deep, slow dubs, typically seen on Tweed? Here, the fish will be lying at far greater depth, and our fly may have to fish at many times the depth we have just mentioned. Of course Tweed

*The ability to wade deep and cast a long line are an integral part of fishing larger rivers.
Spey casting on the Spey at Castle Grant* (Arthur Oglesby)

The Upper Floors beat of the Tweed in autumn: one of the great salmon beats (Arthur Oglesby)

salmon are also to be found in the shallower stretches, but we cannot simply ignore the dubs. On the other hand, the wading fisherman, rather than one using a boat, will spend much of his time on the shallower water fish, simply because it is unlikely that he will be able to cover the deeper lies effectively. Naturally there will be exceptions, where deep water comes close to the bank but, for now, let's stick with the shallower water fish.

Late in October on the Nith – the river still high but clearing nicely, with many of the pools coming into ply for fishing with the fly – the riverside scene screamed 'fish'. Picture a relatively shallow pool, I doubt that the depth reaches 8ft in more than a couple of places. Twin streams rush in at the head, fanning out into a strong flow broken by swirls and whorls; a fine glide gathers momentum toward the shallower tail. At this height of water, you can fish practically the entire length of the pool with confidence.

Standing well up at the head of the pool, I extended my line by 2yd at each cast, until I had something in excess of 20yd out. For the full force of the headstream, I was having to cast well downstream at an acute angle, to slow down the swing of the line. I still wasn't happy that the fly was fishing slowly enough, so I shot some spare, hand-held line into an upstream mend at the very moment that the line alighted on the water. Roll, double Spey and then mend, with two paces between each sequence; I began to work my way down the pool. Soon, I felt slight nudges on the near stationary line, signifying that the fly was touching the bottom in places. I knew I could dispense with the mends. Two casts later, the line simply stopped in its swing. The fight was hard but short and successful; the needle points of the treble hook were deeply embedded in the jaw of 11lb of solid silver – a typical success for cold-water tactics.

The response of a salmon to the stimulus of the fly may depend on a number of factors. These might be defined as anger, curiosity, at least going through the motions of feeding, or whatever. However, as we have to find a peg upon which to hang our hat we could do a lot worse in cold-water fishing than to stick to the idea that we are trying to stimulate a feeding response. If the response we happen to achieve is aggressive – a possibility when salmon become noticeably territorial toward the spawning time – so be it. It will not alter our basic technique.

To initiate the feeding response, our fly must have the appearance of food, in fact to represent a small fish. It certainly looks like a fish with its slim profile, but it must also move like such a creature if the illusion is to be complete. From that basis, it seems that we should endeavour to fish it with a water speed of about 4mph, certainly not much more. This means that, for most of the time, because the fly is fishing across and into the stream, we will have to slow down its passage as much as possible. But it also means that, as the fly swings into slack water, we must maintain its water speed. That is why I prefer to say that the fly should be fished 'at a natural water speed' which is rather different from simply saying 'slow'.

It may not seem all that important whether the fly is swimming fast or slow in terms of lateral movement across the stream, so long as it is not racing upstream;

but the water speed of the fly is the product of both lateral and forward, or backward, movement. You probably remember something of Pythagoras from schooldays, and possibly something of vectors. If a fly is simply hanging stationary in a 3mph current, its water speed is 3mph. However, if it also has lateral movement of 3mph across the current, its resolved water speed is, as near as we need to know, about 4½mph. Equally, if a fly is moving at 3mph across a 4mph current, or vice-versa, its water speed is 5mph. And so, if we are fishing our fly across a stream of anything in excess of about 4mph, accepting that this is getting close to the maximum water speed of which a fish of about 3in length would be capable, we must keep lateral movement, the swing of the line, to a minimum.

Equally important, we should think of how a small fish would be swimming across the stream. If you have ever swum across a current you will know that, if you aim directly at the point where you hope to come ashore, you will be swept away downstream of it. Gundogs that do much work in and across rivers, if

Some aspects of fly control

The water speed of the fly is a combination of lateral movement as well as speed of current. A fly moving at 3mph across a 4mph current has a resolved water speed of 5mph

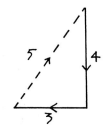

If a belly is allowed to form in the line, the fly will fish unnaturally broadside to the stream

As the fly travels into slacker water, there will be a tendency for it to drop at the tail, unless its water speed is maintained by handlining

they are clever, quickly learn this lesson. And, in just the same way, our fly must keep pointing up into the stream for, if it turns broadside on, it too will be swept away, or should be if it is to appear natural. It is important, therefore, to avoid any downstream belly in the line, which will pull the fly into a beam-on position to the stream.

Finally, the fly should fish on an even keel if it is to maintain its natural appearance. As it swims out of the faster water and into the slack at the side, there will be a natural tendency for it to droop at the tail. For this, and other reasons, it is important to maintain the water speed of the fly, by handlining, as it comes into slacker water.

As discussed in Chapter 5, there are two ways to slow down the passage of the fly. Firstly, we should cast with as long a line as possible and cast well downstream. If we cast squarely, this puts a belly in the line, not only pulling the fly broadside-on to the stream, but also dragging it across. The temptation is ever present, particularly on wider rivers, to cast more squarely in order to cover more water; but it is a hundred times better to cover a smaller area of water effectively than a larger area ineffectively. The way to increase effective water coverage is to cast a longer line and to be prepared to wade deep. Fish do not seem to be unduly disturbed by a wadered body passing close to their lies. There was a sea trout which, when I was fishing the upstream worm in clear water, followed the worm as it trundled back to me. Finally, the fish lifted the worm off the toe of my wader and swam away with its prey. Of course I am not suggesting that we should all start wading through salmons' lies but, if we wade cautiously, there is not too much to fear.

So we cast as long a line as possible at a shallow angle and, where necessary, we are prepared to wade deep in order to extend our effective water coverage. All that is left is to mend the line, incorporating a large, upstream belly. Mending line is normally associated with floating line fishing. After all, as it involves rolling a loop of line into an upstream position, it is obviously impossible to do this unless the line is on the surface. However, we can mend a sinking line, but only at that moment when it is still on the surface, before it sinks. Mending line is also normally associated with controlling the water speed of the fly, but in sunk line fishing we also use it to effect the depth at which the fly is fishing and, again, to extend our effective water coverage.

With some consideration, it is obvious that the fly will not fish at the same depth throughout the whole of the arc of its swing. To begin with, it will be just below the surface and, all other things being equal, it will be fishing at its maximum depth at the end of its swing. For want of a better way of expressing it, if the line sinks at 2in per second, after 10 seconds it will be 20in below the surface, after 20 seconds it will be 40in below, and after 30 seconds it will have sunk to 60in. It is not as simple as that, but it makes the point clear that, for the first part of the swing, the fly may not have reached an effective depth. Putting in a large upstream mend, causing the fly to remain practically in one position, dropping slowly downstream as the line is straightened by the current, gives the

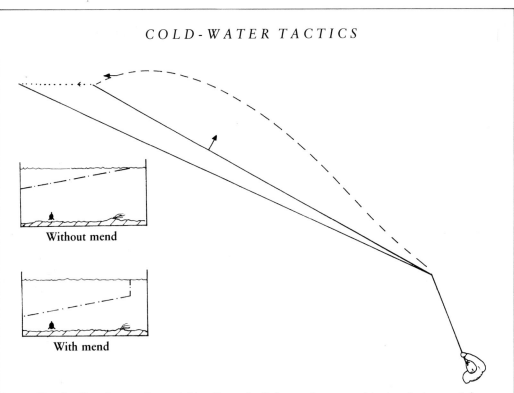

Mending line: by mending a sinking line as it alights on the water, this gives it time to sink as well as slowing its speed

fly and line some time to sink. In this way, we can increase the time and distance at which the fly is fishing at an effective depth.

Mending is difficult enough with a sinking line. It is practically impossible with any line profile other than a double-taper. Line will have been retrieved prior to casting; the bulk of this will be shot as the line uncurls above the water but a yard or two is held back until the moment when the line alights, and then used to create the upstream mend without jerking the fly.

Some fishermen have a tendency to lead the fly around with the rod tip. All this does is speed up the passage of the fly. It is far better to keep the rod tip pointing straight out across the stream. This keeps the centre of the arc of swing as far out as possible, again serving to keep the fly fishing as slowly as possible.

Eventually, the fly will come to the dangle, straight downstream from the rod tip. I have seen it suggested that the fly should now be led, by swinging the rod across the front of the fisherman. In theory, this is perfectly sound. In deep wading in particular, fish may be lying inshore of the wading fisherman. It is the manner of the swing with which I take issue. If the rod is simply swung round on a horizontal plane, the fly will not only swing across, it will also fall back. With a 15ft rod, it will fall back as far as 5yd. And, as the water is probably slacker, this totally defeats our aim to maintain the water speed of the fly. Is it natural for a small fish to swim strongly across a stream and then, as it enters slacker water, to fall away downstream? Surely, as it enters the slack, it should be forging away

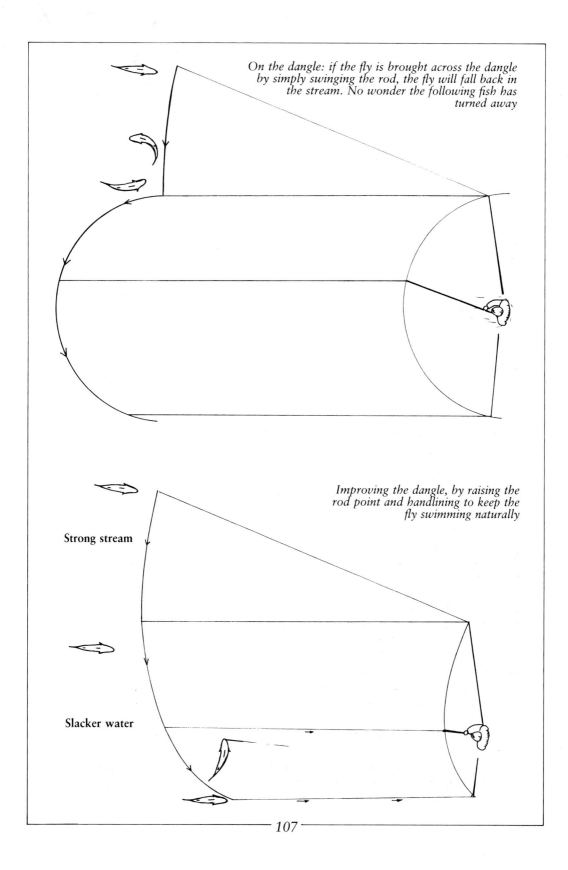

On the dangle: if the fly is brought across the dangle by simply swinging the rod, the fly will fall back in the stream. No wonder the following fish has turned away

Improving the dangle, by raising the rod point and handlining to keep the fly swimming naturally

Strong stream

Slacker water

upstream, not down? And, equally surely, a salmon that has been following the fly – something that salmon seem most likely to do in the coldest water – will be unimpressed with this behaviour, and reject our offering.

It is far better to swing the rod up and across, rather than simply straight across, and to gently draw in some line at the same time, gradually accelerating as the fly swings inshore of the fisherman in order to maintain the water speed. This has the additional benefit of creating some droop in the line from the high-held rod as a cushion to the take of a salmon that takes on the dangle. This is possibly the hardest of all fish to hook cleanly, but a positive take can be encouraged if a little thought is given to maintaining the water speed.

A speed of 4mph is equal to 6ft per second, therefore, as a fly swims out of a 4mph current into one of 2mph, we must accelerate it to maintain its water speed, and this requires us to retrieve line at 3ft per second. Retrieving line at rates such as 1yd per second in a slack current of 2mph, or 2yd per second in still water, certainly does not seem slow, and is another reason why I shy away from describing cold-water tactics as being always deep and slow; but it is a logical speed for the size of fish that we are trying to represent.

Angle of cast We have seen that the way to fish the line and fly slowly is to cast a long line at a relatively shallow angle to the stream. What, exactly, is a 'shallow' angle?

Any cast made at a greater angle than 45 degrees to the bank will be far too square, except in the slackest of water. For the majority of situations, we should be thinking in terms of a maximum not far exceeding 30 degrees, certainly when searching out the cheeks of the mainstreams. This is certainly true of those times when the water temperature remains in the thirties and lower forties. Even when the temperature is higher, when it can make good tactical sense to fish a really long fly in relatively fast water, water speed should not be allowed to become excessive and, therefore, the shallow-angled cast still seems the best alternative.

Lessons can be learnt from harling, when a boat is gently eased across the current while a lively lure such as a Rapala or Kynoch Killer trails far behind on a long line. To my mind it is a deadly dull way of fishing, but it cannot be denied as a highly effective method of catching fish on the fat beats of the lower Tay. Our fly is not going to be hung out behind a boat and left to play in the current while we row, or motor, back and forth across the river and yet, in many ways, that is just the style of presentation we are trying to achieve. The light fly that will work in a limited current is fished across the stream as slowly as possible, and we hope that this produces a lively and attractive stimulus.

Is there any occasion when, in cold-water conditions, the cast is made at a square angle to the stream? Yes there is, because salmon do not always behave as we might wish. There are times, in summer as well as at the cold extremes of the season, when they lie in water where the current is far too slack to fish the fly effectively. In order to fish such stretches we have the alternatives of simply handlining the fly across, or backing-up.

BACKING-UP

Backing-up as a technique of salmon fishing is firmly associated with rivers such as the Thurso, Wick, Brora and others which flow through the low and flat moorland areas of the far north-east of Scotland. But I have seen the technique working well to the south, and often find it the best method to use in fishing a sluggish stretch of water.

The outstanding feature of backing-up is that the pool is fished up, rather than down. Starting at the bottom of the stretch to be fished, a square cast is made across the stream. After a few seconds pause to allow the line and fly to sink, several yards of line are handlined in and then the fisherman immediately takes four or five paces upstream before making another cast. The handlining and walking draw the fly across the river at a steady pace.

A strong breeze is a great help to this method. A downstream wind is better than nothing, but it is the stiff upstream breeze, with wind against current, that puts a fine chop on the surface. It is said that a 6in wave is as good as a 6in rise in water level in bringing fish into a co-operative mood.

It may seem all wrong in theory, dragging the fly behind the line, bringing it up from behind the fish, but there are very few critics of backing-up among those who have seen how productive it can be on slower, almost canal-like, stretches of water. For some reason that I cannot fathom out, backing-up does not work everywhere. I have said that it is a method associated with the far north-east, and it has worked for me as far south as the Annan. And yet, just across the border to the Eden, no more than half-an-hour's drive from the Annan, it will not work. Or so I was assured by Malcolm Dutchman-Smith. Malcolm's home water is the Eden, but he also spends some time on the Thurso each year. It was up there that he learnt the technique of backing-up and he remembers thinking that it seemed ideally suited to some of the long, slow Eden pools. But, try as he might, he could not get it to work on his return home. On the day that we discussed this, we both took fish from slow stretches by gently handlining our flies back through practically still water, and these were welcome fish from a low, slack Eden suffering from a harsh lack of water. But why won't backing-up work there?

Incidentally, a level and relatively uncluttered river bank is by far the easiest platform from which to work the fly in backing-up but, like me, you may find each stone over which to trip, every hole in which to twist an ankle, and each and every tussock of heather on which to catch your line. It is hard to walk backwards, concentrating on line and fly, and still notice these things that are sent to try us. But top marks must go to a friend who, because he is a very well-known fisherman, I shall not embarrass by naming. We were fishing a lowland river together, and the ghillie mentioned that he had heard of backing-up, but never seen it done. The pool looked ideal for the purpose, slow and with a good chop on it, so my friend was not hesitant in volunteering to demonstrate. The river bank must have looked particularly treacherous because he decided to get

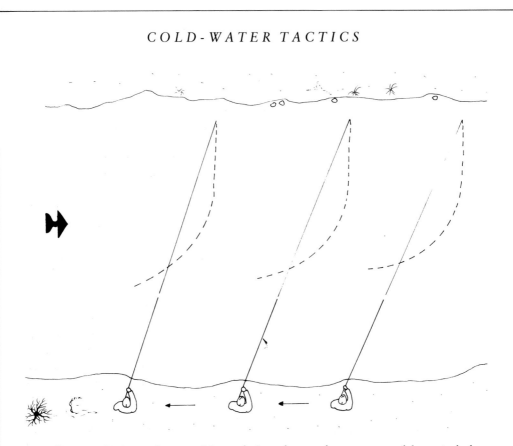

Backing up: this is a rather surprising technique, but can be very successful, particularly in sluggish water

in and wade. Well, everything was going fine. He was casting a really good length of line, covering the pool well, handlining then pacing backward, with the odd cautious glance, for four or five steps at each cast. He must have been feeling rather pleased with himself because I remember he was making some particularly clever pronouncement as to where a fish might take; then he took another pace and disappeared. Luckily the hole wasn't too deep, and he was soon spluttering on the bank, while we rolled about laughing. I don't know, but I doubt whether backing-up ever caught on at that particular beat. Still, it was a good excuse for a dram, if such a thing were ever needed.

BOAT FISHING

When a fisherman stands on the river bank and casts 25yd of line at an angle of 30 degrees to the bank, his fly will pitch into the water about 20yd downstream and rather less than 15yd out from the bank. That may be sufficient to cover most of the fish when they are lying close in to the bank in high water; however, as the water level falls and fish move out further, if the fisherman is to maintain effective water coverage and not fall for the temptation of casting at a square angle, he must be prepared to don chest waders and get in deep.

Even then, on the larger rivers, there will be times when lies in midstream cannot be effectively covered even by the most confident of waders. It is for this prime consideration, as well as various tactical reasons, that many of the beats on our wider salmon rivers are equipped with boats. The boat and boatman are there to ensure that you can cover all the lies effectively; not simply to allow you to fish in the lap of luxury.

Tay boats are normally used for harling, but on Tweed and Spey the boats are used as casting platforms for the fly fisherman. Other rivers have boats as well. On my first visit to the Beauly, I was beginning to think that boats were simply used by the ghillies and fishermen as a convenient way of crossing the river which hardly seemed wide enough to merit their use, but they fish from them as well.

It is interesting to note the differences in methods of boat handling as seen on Spey and Tweed. The normal Spey boat is a craft of some 14ft, slightly longer than a Tweed boat. It is normally worked by rope and anchor. Having rowed the boat out to the chosen position at the head of the pool, the boatman drops the anchor. A good boatman is clever in the way he handles a boat on the rope, the oars playing an important part in the operation; but the basis of the technique is that the boatman lets out a yard or so of rope at the end of each cast, the rope having been neatly wound in a figure of eight on cleats positioned in the bow.

When a fish is hooked, it is a simple matter for the boatman to take the rope, which has been running straight out from the bow, and secure it to a cleat positioned on the side of the boat, someway back from the bow. This turns the bow for the shore, and otters the boat in. With a few strokes on the oars, the fisherman is soon being deposited on the bank from where he plays the fish. Incidentally, the correct method to depart from the boat is to sit on the stern, with your feet dangling in the water, and simply 'shuffle bottom' off.

Tweed boats, not having to face the rapids and rough water of the Spey, are far lighter craft, and generally a foot or so shorter. The fisherman sits astern of the boatman on a round, swivel seat, where he can feel very bossy and master of all he surveys! Tweed boatmen are quite happy to row all day in their shallow-draft boats on the easier Tweed currents. This leads to the most effective water coverage by far. The boatman can introduce all sorts of subtle variations to the fly presentation, letting the boat drift here, easing it laterally across the current there; even backing-up. Tweed boat fishing is very much a partnership. A good boatman will quickly gauge the ability of his fisherman and act accordingly, and he can make all the difference between success and failure.

Unlike on the Spey, Tweed boatmen prefer to row their boat toward the bank when a fish is hooked, but they hold the boat slightly offshore until they feel happy that the fish is well controlled. The boat is then taken to the bank where the boatman gets ashore with his big net, but the fisherman is expected to remain on his seat and fight the fish from there. After all, if the fish does set off on a

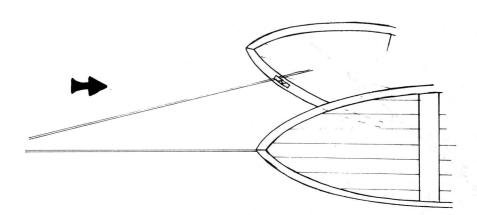

Ottering: by moving the rope to a side cleat, the boat's bows are forced out into the stream

searing run, it is far easier to follow in the boat than stumble along the bank, and it is only seconds work to push-off and get back on the oars.

Another boating technique, used on both rivers, is for the boatman to remain on the bank and let his fisherman down on a rope; or rather he lets the boat down with the fisherman in it. We are back to the manoeuvre known as ottering, as described for bringing the boat ashore on the Spey. Much depends upon the set of the current, but it can be a killing method. When a fish is hooked, the boatman heaves on the line and pulls the boat ashore, a job made so much easier if the fisherman has the forethought to free the line from its inboard cleat. For the Tweed boatman, certainly, it must come as a welcome break from constantly rowing on a day of strong downstream winds.

Boat fishing offers maximum scope for the use of a shooting-head, the coils of oval monofilament backing stowed at the fisherman's feet prior to each cast. On the dark and mysterious dubs of lower Tweed, a very fast sinking shooting-head will get a fly well down, and this deep-water fishing can be startlingly productive. This type of fishing reminds me a little of the tactics I employ for sea trout in the darkest hours of summer nights when big fish can be tempted to take a fly inched back through the depths. The fast-sinking line is cast out across the slow-moving water at a relatively shallow angle, the boat providing the ideal casting platform. Wishing the line, leader and fly 'bon voyage', you wait many seconds before gently working the fly back. Is it really fly fishing? Maybe not, but it is a useful ace to carry up your sleeve.

In a suitable current, a boatman can stay ashore and 'otter' his boat and fisherman down the pool

7

WARM-WATER TACTICS

The most prominent trend in salmon behaviour, as it concerns the fisherman, is that the fish will show a preference for a fly that is fishing close to the surface when the water temperature exceeds 50°F or thereabouts. Many authorities have also suggested that they also prefer a smaller fly than those associated with cold-water tactics. That is true, in general terms, but there are times when long flies are still more than able to tempt fish, even with the temperature well up in the fifties.

FLOATER OR INTERMEDIATE LINE

Where I seem to be at odds with many fishermen is that I am not convinced that the floating line is always the best tackle for presenting a fly just below the surface. There are two alternatives: either a fairly heavy fly fished below a floater, or a lighter fly fished above a slow sinker – probably a neutral density, intermediate line. Both techniques end up with a fly fishing at the same depth and I use both, according to circumstances.

Floating line is seen as the traditional method of presentation, the modern technique having grown out of 'greased line'; but the light fly and sinking line method is just as deeply rooted in history. It was originally known as the 'oiled-line' technique, as developed by Alexander Grant. Grant was a no-nonsense

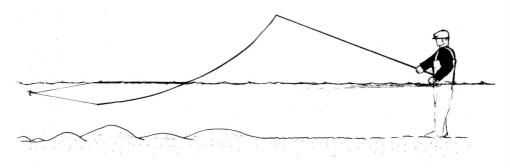

Floater or intermediate? To fish a fly just below the surface, the fisherman has the choice of a light fly above an intermediate line, or a rather heavier fly below a floater

Essence of summer salmon on the floating line, and ghillie Gabriel McKay nets a salmon for the late Teddy Bentley

Highlander who corresponded with Einstein and revelled in such matters as the fourth dimension, dynamics, mathematics and a dozen other 'ics'. When he put his active mind to the problems of salmon-fishing tackle and technique, he decided firmly against the floating line. Grant's beliefs and techniques are described in the book *Fine and Far Off* by Jock Scott. With the introduction of the modern, intermediate line, I have attempted to put the method into a modern context.

The thinking behind the technique is to reduce any possibility of alarming a fish, hence the title, we fish 'fine and far off'. Grant accepted that thousands of fish are caught on the floating line, but he argued that it might put down others: 'no fish would like to see a big, black snake floating over its head – and the line would look dark to a fish looking up at it against the light.' Here lies the hint as to when and where to fish the intermediate, and I think Grant was wrong to insist that we should never fish with a floater. Certainly I prefer to fish the intermediate in times of low, clear water and bright sunshine, for example the Aberdeenshire Dee when its renowned gin-clear water runs low and hot under a cloudless sky. But picture a river like the Spey, or any river running at 2ft on the gauge after a 6ft rise, the pools in marvellous ply for the fly and plenty of cloud cover; what worries can there be then in fishing the floater?

To sum up, I see the need for both lines as applied to warm-water tactics. There have been times in the past when I may have been guilty of overstating the case for the intermediate. If so, I apologise for it. Is it not inevitable when attempting to revive or introduce a new method upon a thoroughly conservative scene? I have to admit that if I was forced to make a choice between floater or intermediate for the rest of my warm-water salmon fishing, I would probably choose the floater. It casts so pleasantly, no other line handles so well; it is a joy to fish with. But how I would hate to be forced into a stereotyped approach, and the use of an intermediate line has so much logic behind it. I like the theoretical arguments for the light fly fished above an intermediate line. They are an extension of my thinking on the 'balloon effect' that I apply to cold-water fishing. The light and active fly darts and hovers, reacting to the stream, with every semblance of life. In practice, it proves every bit as attractive as it does in theory.

Beside choice of line, there are other tackle changes that I make in using this technique. The salmon lines I use on the double-handed rod are those manufactured by Masterline. They claim to have the finest tips available in order to give a sweet turnover and gentle presentation to the fly. I maintain this fine taper in the leader, using either a full-length Normark Adapta Leader, all 16ft of it, tapering down to a 7lb point for the smallest flies, or cut a foot or so off the tip to increase the breaking strain and diameter when fishing rather larger flies. Another style of leader I really like for this fishing is one of the extra-steep tapers. These are 9ft leaders, and so I knot an extra length of level nylon, about 5ft long, to the tip.

I suspect you may be saying 'fuss and nonsense' about this technique but, believe me, by getting the line below the surface and using a long leader to keep the line well away from the fly, more fish will be taken in low, clear water, in bright conditions – the type of situation that we may have to endure for long periods in the summer months.

Being a sunk-line technique, however, it is almost totally reliant on deep wading and long casting in terms of the wider rivers. It limits our effective water coverage. Equally, it has to be said that an intermediate is not nearly so pleasant a line to cast as the floater. And the arguments for fishing a light and active fly are almost irrelevant when fishing a good push of streamy water, where any but the heaviest fly will have plenty of action about it anyway.

CHOICE OF FLY

It has already been stressed that the choice of fly is extremely important; therefore although I have already written at some length on the choice of size and design, it will not go amiss to say a little more.

Most fishermen would accept that the larger flies we fish in cold-water conditions are caricatures of small fish. However, what the smaller flies represent, nobody can say for sure. It certainly seems unlikely that any form of crustacean or plankton could swim across a 6mph current in the headstreams of a pool, so are they really nothing more than a suggestion of something good to eat, with neither we, nor possibly the salmon, exactly sure what that something might be?

When discussing the choice of size for a salmon fly, we all talk largely in terms of water temperature; but it is equally true that the faster the water being fished, the larger our fly must be. This kills stone-dead the argument that size in relation to temperature may be due to salmon associating a certain size of prey with ocean currents of similar temperature to that which they are experiencing in the river. Otherwise, we would always fish the same size of fly at a given temperature, regardless of the speed of the water.

Theorists of the 'greased-line school' and subsequently of the floating line, will suggest that the fly size to use can be reduced to a formula, equating temperature with speed, height and clarity of the water. But A. H. E. Wood seemed to disregard these factors: Wood's thoughts are given in *Greased Line Fishing* by Jock Scott. 'As long as the fish will come for a No 6, I do not go lower. I only reduce the size of fly as the fish becomes shy of the larger sizes in small hooks.' Nowadays there is a tendency toward the use of long-winged flies, not necessarily the super-long patterns such as the Collie Dog, but more standard hair-wing patterns, such as the Munro Killer, where the wing is extended to 1½ or 2 times the length of the body. In fact, these are not all that new and Edward Hewitt, in his book *Secrets of the Salmon*, describes flies of 2½in length tied on No 6 hooks on which he often caught fish after having unsuccessfully tried standard patterns. Was it that there was something particularly attractive about these long-winged flies, or was it simply that the standard patterns were not long enough? And it should be noted that we tend to fish a long-wing tied on the same-sized hook as we used previously for a standard pattern. In other words, we stick to fishing, for example, a size 6 regardless of whether its overall length is 1in or 2in!

It is correct, I am sure, to pay close attention to the water temperature when choosing the size of fly with which to fish, but equally important is the height and speed of the water and, also, the nature of the river. For example, if the water temperature is a little over 50°F, our standard choice will be toward a size 6. But when, say, we are fishing a strong and powerful river, we increase the size of fly. And if the river is running high, we increase the size a little more, and for fishing a fast stream up goes the size again. The logical choice seems to be for a big fly, say a long-wing tied on a size 2 or 4 hook, or possibly one of the articulated flies more readily associated with cold-water fishing. And I have seen salmon caught on Collie Dogs with wings in excess of 6in so many times in such conditions that I must include them as another possibility.

Now consider a similar temperature of about 50°F on a smaller river in fairly low, clear and slow water. Down, down, down goes the size until we eventually settle on a size 10. So, the temperature/size relationship is the easy part of the

These salmon fell for a size 6 fly; sometimes suggested as the 'standard' summer size

equation. After that, it takes a nicety of judgement to decide the final size of fly, and the proportions of hook to wing length and so on. I am not alone in thinking that, at the end of the day, we fish the fly in which we have the most confidence. We have a hunch that this is the fly that will bring success. But for an experienced fisherman to pass on this knowledge is like trying to explain what makes for 'good hands' in riding a horse!

Having discussed what size of fly to use, using temperature to decide the standard size, and then adjusting this in accordance with the nature of the river, its height and the speed of the particular stretch it is intended to fish, and having devoted another section to thoughts on fly design, let me turn to the question of pattern. Do you remember those egg-rolling gulls that fascinated Baerends and Krujit by showing a preference for oversized, bright-green dummy eggs rather than natural ones? Nobody can say why this should have been so, any more than one can say exactly why a salmon may show a preference for one fly rather than another. I do not know if our scientists returned the next year to see if the gulls still preferred that particular style of dummy egg, and whether the gulls of another colony, hundreds of miles away, showed the same preference. But I do know that, in my travels to many rivers in counties from Cornwall to Caithness, from the east coast of Scotland to the western seaboard of Ireland, time after time I have met fisherman of wide and deep experience who insist that, on their particular river, the salmon prefer a certain pattern of fly. I have heard so many instances where fishermen have strongly believed that a change of pattern was material in the taking of fish. Who am I to be so conceited as to say 'stuff and nonsense' to them all. In my own locality, fishermen who have known both rivers all their lives will insist that a dark fly is the pattern for the Nith, but a fly with a touch of yellow will serve better on the Annan. And when the ghillie on a beat, whose father and grandfather were ghillies before him, tells me that a certain pattern of fly works well, should I ignore his words entirely? Of course not! On the other hand, having tried the local favourites, this does not mean that we are not free to experiment as we see fit.

I really cannot see why some people feel it is impossible that there is any advantage in one pattern over another at a given place, at a given time, in certain conditions, simply because nobody can give any firm ruling as to why this should be so. It is a pity that we cannot explain it better, but our own experience builds upon that of generations of countless thousands of salmon fishermen to create a picture of 'what, where and when' that I am not prepared to deny.

PRESENTATION

The presentation of a salmon fly is very largely a matter of fishing the fly at the appropriate angle, speed and depth. The experience of generations has shown that, in warm-water conditions, the fly will produce the greatest response when fished close to the surface, say roughly within the top 6in, but not so close that a fish will necessarily have to show in the take. That leaves us with angle and speed which are so closely linked that they may be considered as one and the same thing. And, surely, all the rules that we applied to large flies on sinking lines for cold-water tactics, in order to make the fly appear natural must, if anything, be even more important when it comes to warm-water techniques.

It doesn't seem reasonable to worry about the water speed of a 3in fly fishing across relatively slack water, then not show equal concern when it comes to fishing a far smaller fly across faster water associated with the temporary resting places of salmon in warm water. Again we are seeing the need for reducing the water speed of the fly as far as possible by a shallow-angled cast and, in order to maximise our water coverage on wider rivers, the need to be able to wade deep and cast a long line. Mending line can be useful but should be kept to a minimum, particularly on areas of unbroken water, glides etc.

But that's enough of this theorising. Let's go fishing and, just for a pinch of originality, let's not go to the Spey yet again, however wonderful that particular river may be. Instead, let us travel to one of the medium-sized rivers where so much sport is enjoyed, but where it is not so dependent on long casting and deep wading although these accomplishments may still be important. In Scotland we have a wealth of such rivers to choose from: Beauly, Brora, Helmsdale and Lochy to the north, Findhorn and Upper Dee in the north-east, rivers such as the North and South Esks and Earn in the east, the Awe in the west, and the Nith in

A small but lively fish on the Lochy

the south-west, among others. We shall not worry whether it is late May or early September, only that the water temperature is in the lower fifties and that the river has fallen to 2ft on the gauge and cleared after a 6ft rise following a spate.

So, here we are at the head of a nice looking pool. Before we do anything else, let's remember the words of the late John Ashley Cooper when he said that one of the things that sets apart the successful fisherman is attention to detail. You will have already unwound your fly line, a floater in these conditions, in order to check the splice between it and the backing – a needle-knot if you are using monofilament backing as I do, and re-wound your line carefully onto the spool. Tape the joints of your rod with insulating tape, it is embarrassing to have your rod tip sail off; and tape the reel fitting as well if it is one of those simple, sliding-ring affairs. Check all your knots, and now it is time to choose a fly.

With the water temperature in the lower fifties, a size 6 will be the standard from which to work. The river is of medium size, so make no adjustment for its nature; but it is running fairly high, so we shall increase the size a little and, because the pool that you are about to fish contains some fairly fast streams in the head and tail, why not settle on a size 4 standard double, with a fairly long wing? As to pattern, it is a fairly dull day and as you have heard that the Munro Killer takes its share of fish in these parts, you would do well to start with that.

Will you need to change the size of fly as you fish down the pool? Some fishermen would use the size 4 for the headstreams then, as the current slackens into the body of the pool, change down to a size 6, or a 4 with a standard length of wing. Then they would use a size 6 for the slower middle section, or a long-winged 8. What a carry on! We know that these changes are made in the belief that we must vary the size of the fly in order to suit the current speed and to ensure that the fly stays fishing at roughly the same depth. However, we also know that we can adjust the water speed of the fly by varying the angle of our cast. In order to increase the water speed, we need only cast a little squarer, and this maintains the depth because it is the water speed of the fly, not the speed of the current, that affects its buoyancy, ie the speed at which the water flows over, through and under the hackle, wing and body.

So now you fish the pool down, taking care to make a long, downstream cast in the headstream, gradually casting a little more square as you enter slower water, and then reducing the angle as you start to fish into the gathering momentum of the tail. Nothing happens. The question now arises as to whether to move on, or to try another cast down the pool. It looks so 'fishy' that you decide to give it another go. But this time you decide to replace the size 4 with a 6 and to fish it as slowly as possible, throwing in a big mend as well as casting well downstream in the faster sections. As you approach the tail, just as your fly is slowly hovering and working across that roughly broken section of water close to the boulder that juts proud of the surface, your line stops. The reel clicks. You stay cool as it accelerates into the whirring song of the ratchet then, just as the

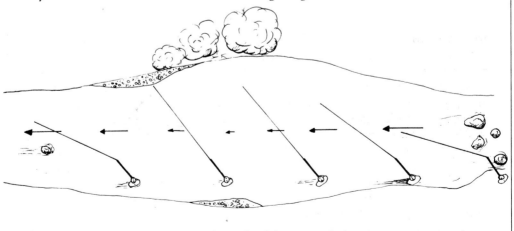

Adjusting the angle: by increasing the angle of the cast in slacker streams, water speed is maintained and there is no need to change the size of fly

music subsides, you clamp the line to the rod and feel for the deep thrumming of the fish. Five minutes later, you net out a fine, fresh fish of 9lb.

As an alternative to the smaller fly fished slower you might, of course, have chosen a larger fly and fished it faster. The fly might have been a small member of the Collie Dog family. Small in Collie terms, but still having a wing of 3in whipped to a ¾in brass tube. Such a fly can produce particularly exciting sport at dusk in the streams right up in the neck of the pool. Salmon move up to breathe freely in the oxygenated water, or in response to the urge to run; probably a little of both. Getting well upstream and almost harling the fly, fishing it on a long line at the dangle, moving it slowly back and forth across the stream, can produce a taking fish. But even on outpoint trebles, such a take is not always easy to convert into a solid hooking.

When fishing down the pool in the normal way, you may be concerned as to what distance to move between casts. I like to get a move on. On a big, long Spey pool I would think nothing of taking three paces between casts and, on a smaller river, probably two. It is only in times of coloured water that I would reduce to one pace between casts. And I do mean paces, not tentative shuffles. There is only one time that you will see me stop when fishing down a pool, and it is about to happen to you.

We left you admiring that fish, but now you are fishing another pool. Your fly was swinging round when you felt a distinct twitch and then nothing more. It might have been a fish – a salmon. Advice on what to do when you believe that a salmon has merely nudged at your fly is varied, to say the least. My own solution is to stay exactly where I am, but to strip in line so that the fly is hanging in the stream just a few yards below me, and I hold the line in coils. I like to rest the fish, passing the time by smoking a cigarette, although now that I am supposed to have given up smoking I shall have to carry some slabs of very chewy toffee. I pull up the fly, change it for something a little larger, and check my knots, the points of the hooks and so on. It may be that a hook point has broken off on the original fly, although this is extremely rare when Spey casting; or it may be that the leader has caught between the hooks and the fly has been fishing back to front. In either of these cases, I would not change the size, style or pattern of fly.

Cigarette smoked, or toffee chewed, I let the current work out the line straight downstream and then cast, knowing that the fly will swing back on the same arc that produced the nudge but, with the larger fly, I cast a little more square and this makes it fish faster. If, after three casts, I have had no response, I pull in line, change the fly to something smaller and, after a suitable pause, cast at a shallower angle, fishing rather slower but still across that same arc. If still nothing, I fish down the pool in the normal way. My thinking is that the fish is one of those teetering on the brink between its normal, non-taking behaviour and disinhibition. By altering the stimulus just slightly, I hope to give the fish that little extra nudge that seemed to be lacking in the original fly and presentation. On a day when fish are scarce, it seems a pity not to make the most of such an obvious sign from a salmon.

You will now see that there is really very little difference between the presentation of a shallow swimming fly off a floating line, and a large fly off a sinking line. Indeed, much of what I said in regard to cold-water tactics and techniques is equally applicable to both situations, for example, fishing the fly across the dangle. The change is really only in terms of depth, rather than angle and water speed, although the floating line does offer a fine degree of line and fly control that is absent from the sinking line.

But you have had enough fun fishing the floating line in a nice height of water. Let's make the going a little tougher, the water a little warmer and lower, and see what changes we can make in terms of technique in order to tempt fish in these less fortuitous conditions.

CONTROLLED DRAG

The major techniques of salmon fishing in either cold or warm water are concerned with casting the fly well downstream and fishing it as slowly as possible. However, there are other methods which, whilst contradicting these general rules, can be deadly as regards catching fish. One of these is the controlled drag.

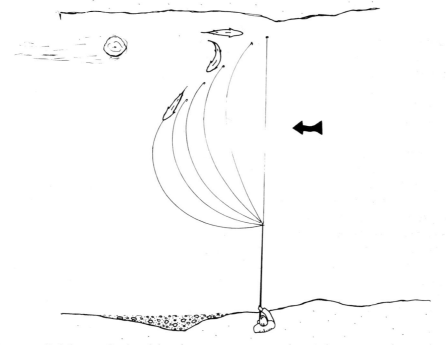

Controlled drag: a fly that fishes downstream into a salmon's lie can provoke a strong, predatory response; but beware of foul-hooking

Controlled drag was devised and used by Percy Laming at the close of last century. He killed a total of approximately 4,500 salmon in his fishing career and, in the days when such things were considered as notable and credit worthy, had such single day takes as 21, 19, 17 and 15 twice, with many other double-figure scores. Probably of greater interest to the modern fisherman was that he refused to be stereotyped in his approach to salmon fishing.

Percy Laming believed and proved that a fly dragging downstream will move and attract fish. The basis of his technique was a very square cast, creating immediate belly in the line. He used it in low, warm water. He may also be said to have invented the sink-tip line in that he used a line that was greased for all but the last 2yd. A modern anti-skate line fishes in just the same way. I like to fish with one of my light, low-water doubles when employing this technique. A pattern such as the Bourrach has plenty of flash, and has served me well, normally a size 6 or 8.

This method should be considered as a technique in its own right, rather than an excuse for making a squarer cast in standard, floating-line practice. In a way, it is probably eliciting a predatory, almost aggressive type of response, rather than simply inducing the fish to go through the motions of feeding. The takes are usually positive and can be quite savage; and it certainly seems that the faster the fly is dragged the better. It is possible to fish the fly too quickly, and a fish may be seen to give chase, snap at the fly, but miss. In such a case, fish the fly rather slower. Takes come on the pursuit, rather than being interceptory. The fly is dragged downstream past the fish, which then sets off after it.

What has happened to all my talk about controlling the water speed of the fly? For here we are with a fly streaking away downstream. The point is that it is only streaking in relation to the river bank and ourselves. Travelling downstream at, say, 9mph relative to the bank, its actual water speed will only be 3mph if the current is flowing at 6mph. Let's not forget that creatures swim downstream as well as up!

This method provides an alternative to fishing tiny flies in low, clear, warm water. It whips a fairly large fly across the fish's vision and, without time for a close inspection, the fish responds immediately by pursuing it, and is committed. If I have an objection to its use, it is that it can very easily lead to the foul-hooking of fish, particularly when they are concentrated in pools during conditions of low water; so it is a method only to be used in the right hands in the right place. It is akin, in many ways, to upstream spinning with a tiny Mepps spoon in similar conditions.

RIFFLING

There was a time when British naval officers were frequent visitors to Newfoundland. As is the way of things, they left some of their treasured salmon flies as presents for their hosts on rivers such as the Portland Creek. After a time, the gut-eyes of such traditional flies became suspect. But rather than throw the fly away, the locals added a knot, tied to the neck of the hook just behind the eye and in front of the wing, for added security. This became known as the Newfoundland hitch.

The problem was that, as anybody who is familiar with the ottering of a boat across a stream will appreciate, when the line was no longer secured to the point of the hook, or rather the eye, the fly was pulled off-balance and would rise to, and cut a wake along, the surface of the water as it fished back. It riffled across the surface. However, the locals quickly realised that, rather than creating a problem, these flies were actually rather good at tempting fish. And so the technique of riffling, employing a Newfoundland hitch on the fly, was born. And today, though probably still more prevalent in North America, British fishermen are coming more and more to realise the value of riffling a fly in times of low water and difficult fishing conditions.

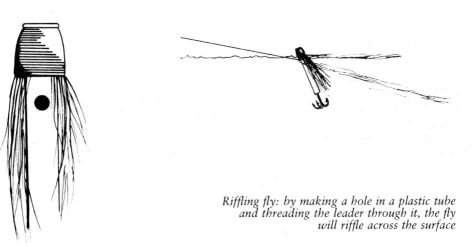

Riffling fly: by making a hole in a plastic tube and threading the leader through it, the fly will riffle across the surface

Personally, I do not bother with the Newfoundland hitch. What I do is take a plastic tube and drill a hole in it with a stout needle, just behind the completed head of the fly. Applying a lit match to the needle while it is still inserted in the tube, ensures that the hole will stay open after the needle is withdrawn. It is now a simple matter to tie up the tube in the conventional way, but leaving a gap in the wing to give access to the hole into which the leader is inserted. I do not dress the body of the fly, and a tuft of black hair is as good as anything for the wing. Such a fly, cast at a fairly square angle, comes riffling back across the surface, cutting a wake which can be as deadly to a salmon in low, warm water as it can be to a sea trout in the darkest hours of the night. It is another useful ace to carry up your sleeve, armed with a small outpoint treble.

(overleaf) Summertime on the Spey, a time when it may pay to vary techniques

DIBBLING A DROPPER

If we choose to fish with a dropper, we should have a certain plan in mind. Some fishermen employ a dropper all the time, probably in response to the difficulties they see in choosing the right size of fly; it allows them to fish, say, a 6 on the dropper and an 8 on the point, separated by about 4ft of nylon on a 10ft cast. I do this sometimes, but am strongly aware of the dangers involved. If a fish is hooked on the dropper and is then allowed to sulk, the trailing fly on the point may catch on the river bottom. Fish have been known to take the spare fly while another fish is already attached to the other, among other hazards.

However, there is a method of fishing the dropper that can be very successful on certain waters. It is known as dibbling and is another method to try in low, summer water. It involves fishing a hair-winged fly, say a size 6 or smaller, tied on a double or Esmond Drury type treble, so that it dibbles along the surface. It is obviously a short-line method and, the longer the rod, the further the dibble can be taken. In many ways, it is the same technique that we use to fish a bob fly on a loch. I say a hair-winged fly, but it might equally be an Elver fly with its long, trailing wing of vulturine guinea-fowl; and I have even heard of fish being taken on a Collie Dog, although I should think that the normal brass tube might be exchanged for one of plastic if the fly were being tied with this technique specifically in mind.

Dibbling a dropper: a method to use in headstreams when the river flows low and warm

This method I firmly associate with fishing broken water right up in the necks of pools. More than that, it seems a method that can only be counted upon on rivers north of the Great Glen and in the Hebrides, although it can, at times, produce fish further south. I tend to use it with my long but light single-handed rod of 12ft and an AFTM 5 floater. This is a very pleasant rod to fish with, but I wonder whether I might do better still to fish with a rod of 15ft, possibly a rod like the late Bill McEwan's Long Lomond that he designed for loch fishing – a 15ft double-handed rod rated AFTM 5–7. Such a length and rating would give fine water coverage with sensitivity. Salmon that come to the dibbled fly are notoriously difficult to hook. The fish must normally be given plenty of time to turn down with the fly.

THE SURFACE FLY

Some will question why I have chosen to refer to the 'surface' rather than the 'dry' fly. The reason is simple. The longer we associate the surface-fly technique for salmon with that of the dry fly as used for trout à la chalkstream, the longer it will take to come to grips with this fascinating branch of the sport.

I used to regard the very rare tales I heard of salmon taking a dry fly, say a Mayfly on the Itchen, as like a dog that walks on its hind legs; not that it does it well but surprising that it does it at all! Americans came over to see if they could take Scottish fish on the dry fly, as they take fish at home, but met with very little success. But then I started to hear of more and more salmon and grilse being taken off flies fished on the surface, nearly all from the spate waters of the Hebrides and Highlands, and my interest was stirred. I decided to give it a try. At the time, we were living in Argyll and this gave me access to a number of suitable rivers; now that we have returned to the Borders, I look forward to returning north-west in order to continue my attempts. To date, they have not produced many fish, but those that I have caught have been tremendously exciting and satisfying. However, they have not been enough to allow me to speak with authority on the subject. Yet, reading everything I can find on the subject combined with speaking to other fishermen who have tried the techniques involved, certain common factors begin to emerge.

Let us look at the conditions that seem most suited to the use of the surface fly. It immediately becomes apparent that this is a method associated with those times when spate rivers are falling away toward their bare bones and fish have adopted long-term lies. A stiff breeze to ruffle the surface of the water is an advantage, just as a sun blazing down from a clear sky is a definite disadvantage.

It seems to be generally accepted that the best fly to use is a tiny, hair-wing dressing on a plastic tube, tiny being from as small as ¼in to a little over ½in in size of tube, creating a fly that will be slightly longer with up to about ¾in of dressing. Such tubes are armed with minute trebles; down to a size 20, I have seen suggested. The Yellow Dolly, created by Derek Knowles, is far and away the best-known fly for the purpose. Tied on a red tube, a collar of stiff yellow hair is tied in at the tail end, over a ridge of silk in order to ensure that the hair splays out. The hair is then trimmed fairly short, to about ¼in on the ½in tube, and you now have something resembling a bristly little sweep's brush. Now we turn to the head and again we tie in a ridge of black silk, over which we tie black hair, rather thinner than the yellow hair at the tail. After securing with a whip finish and varnishing, the black hair is trimmed to finish on a level with the skirt of yellow hair.

Tying this fly is a fiddly little job to perform, but is well worthwhile. Alternatives are a Muddler Minnow, with its head of clipped deer hair, also tied on a tube because nothing hooks and holds so well as those tiny treble hooks. But if you have neither Yellow Dolly or Muddler, you can take comfort from the fact that I have caught fish on a fairly standard Stoat Tail, tied with bucktail on a similar length of tube to the Dolly, and the wing clipped so that it does not extend much behind the tail of the tube.

As to the rest of the tackle, opinions range fairly widely from standard dry-fly rods as used for trout, up to 15ft rods designed for use with light lines, the latter normally being used to fish downstream for, as we shall see, the surface fly can be fished in all directions. The fish I have caught have been on my 12ft single-handed loch rod. I very definitely prefer to fish single-handed in this technique and the extra length allows far greater control of the line as it fishes back from upstream, simply raising the rod tip to maintain contact. And this rod can cast a good length of light line, normally AFTM 5, which settles lightly on the water up to 20yd. Some fishermen who use the technique successfully are happy to fish with 10ft or 12ft of level nylon as a leader. Personally, I prefer a 9ft steep-tapered leader, to which I attach a point of about 2ft of level nylon, 6lb breaking strain. And there we are, ready to start fishing.

If it were ever true that time spent in reconnaissance is never wasted, it is in the case of fishing the surface fly to salmon. The trout is easy meat by comparison, betraying its presence by rising to natural insects, unlike the salmon. An intimate knowledge of the lies of the salmon in the river, together with much belly-crawling and peering with polarised glasses, will establish where and whether a fish is in residence. We can then slither back, without daring to show the merest glimpse of ourselves, and decide how we are to set about catching it. And it is here that I hope you see a little method in my madness. We have just been looking at other recognised methods of taking salmon in low, warm water: controlled drag, the riffling fly and the dibbled dropper. It is from these techniques, far more than anything the trout fisherman can show us, upon which the emergent techniques of fishing the surface fly seem to depend.

Let us presume, in order to make a start, that a strong, downstream breeze is gusting down the glen. If for no other reason than that it will be so very difficult to present the fly well into the teeth of the breeze, we decide on a downstream presentation. The fish, we have seen, is lying slightly out from the opposite bank. Having greased up the fly to ensure that it will float, we wriggle into position, keeping our heads well below the sky-line, staying well back from the bank, and

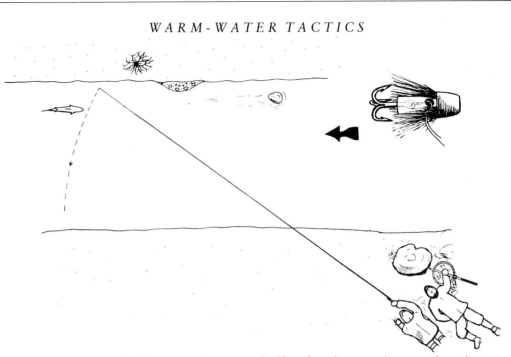

Downstream surface fly: using a tiny, greased riffling fly, salmon can be tempted to take the surface fly

accepting that we shall have to cast at maximum range in order to reduce the possibility that the fish may see us.

When that little fly plops onto the water, hard into the bank, and starts swimming across the surface, leaving a slight wake, it is obviously creating a very similar, if not identical, stimulus to that of the riffled fly or, indeed, the dibbled dropper. The fact that the tiny surface fly is creating far less disturbance is a reflection of the fact that we are fishing water where subtlety is at a premium, and all that is required. Indeed, if the water is fairly fast, I cannot believe that it would make all that amount of difference whether we fished the fly greased, or in the riffling style. There is a point to be made here because I really do not like the floating leader, particularly on a day when there is not total cloud cover. It was with this in mind that I tied up some tiny tubes in the riffling style with a hole just behind the head through which to thread the leader, and with bucktail wings clipped to extend just beyond the tube as in the Dolly. Well greased but fished off a leader treated to sink, such a fly of about ¾in length has produced fish in fairly streamy water. Not a lot of fish but the idea is worthy of consideration.

The main alternative to downstream presentation is upstream and across. Some authorities suggest greasing everything – fly, leader and line; but I find this unnecessary and, probably representing no more than a hangover from dry fly for trout, I do not like a floating leader. I do not see the purpose of it, particularly in bright weather. And, because I know the tiny sizes of trout flies that I can keep floating in rough water above a sunk leader, even fishing small sedge-flies with a degree of drag, I cannot see that it is required to ensure that the fly floats.

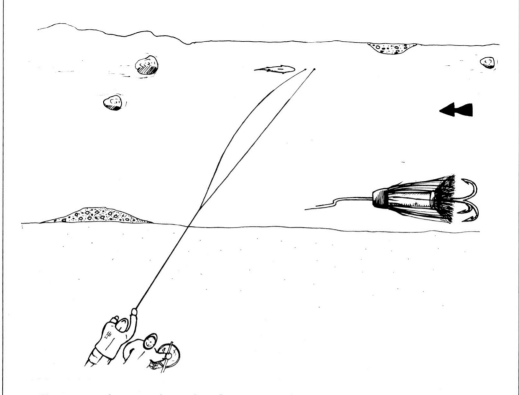

Upstream and across: the surface fly is in its infancy in Britain, but results from the Highlands and Islands are giving great encouragement

The presentation is very similar to that of controlled drag although, if anything, the fly is cast rather more upstream. In controlled drag, it is possible to take fish as the fly skims just below and bulging the surface and so, by presenting a smaller fly on the surface, we create a similar stimulus. Drag can be introduced, but it is wrong to overdo it; just introduce enough so that the fly is fishing ever so slightly faster than the stream.

I would not like to say anything more about fishing the surface fly for salmon. The sport is still very much in its infancy in this country, and we are all still feeling our way. However, if you avoid associating it too readily with the technique of fishing dry fly to trout, with which it has very little in common, and if the few words I have offered act as encouragement to experiment with the method, I shall be satisfied.

I cannot help thinking that this is a method with great appeal for those already keen on deer stalking on the high hills. You must stalk a salmon with the surface fly, often down on your hands and knees. Move gently but purposefully, like a flower opening, wear drab clothing, and keep your profile below the sky-line. Avoid false casting and beware of lining a fish. In short, do all in your power to ensure that the salmon is aware of absolutely nothing other than that tiny fly.

8

LET BATTLE COMMENCE

HOOKING FISH

There can be times when, after a long period of inactivity on the salmon river, we almost forget that our primary purpose is to hook a fish, then to play and land it with maximum efficiency in minimum time. Yes, there is more to fishing than catching fish, but let's not pretend that hooking, playing and landing such a marvellous fish as the salmon is not crucial to our enjoyment of the sport.

Before anything can be said in regard to the hooking of salmon, thought must be given to the way in which they take. If salmon were always to take in the way we chose, there would be no cause for worry; the fish would simply hook themselves. And, on a large number of occasions, that is exactly what happens.

The fish that takes well, and practically hooks itself, is the one that turns in the take. By that I mean that the fish sweeps in from the side and, as it takes the fly, immediately turns downstream.

I was fishing a tremendous pool with a strong push of water down through the body and into the glide and tail. The fly was swimming steadily across when suddenly it was seized, and line was ripped off the reel. Nothing could have been simpler than to grip the line to the rod handle and raise the rod tip into a strong fish which ran vigorously, then ran some more, and finally settled down for a less showy struggle. A few minutes later, as I admired its silvery body laid out on the river bank, I wished that all my salmon would take in such a way. It had positively engulfed the Brora fly.

I largely associate such takes with warmer water temperatures. Salmon are more active than in the coldest water conditions and, on the whole, if a salmon wants a fly and is really committed in the take, it will seldom make a mistake. We are fishing the fly just below the surface. It might be late May or early June, or later on in September. Salmon will be responding well in the warm, but not too warm, water. They turn well in the take, often bulging the surface as they do so. The floating line jumps taut off the water, throbbing as the fish pulls hard against the spring of the rod. It all happens so cleanly that there can be little doubt as to whether the hook is well set.

Such takes can be considered as pursuit takes, where the fly has passed in front of the salmon, or interceptory where the salmon has seen the fly as it approaches

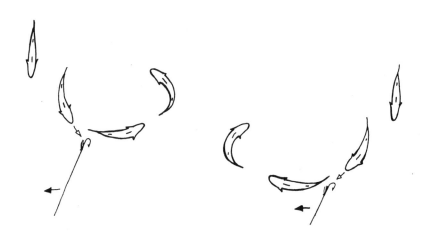

Interceptory and pursuit takes, but the difference is largely academic because, either way, the salmon practically hooks itself when it turns positively

and moves forward to meet it. These distinctions are little more than academic. The important point is that the fish turns as it takes, ensuring a secure hook hold. The fish has taken the fly and turned back to its lie in one glorious movement.

My own approach to hooking these warm-water salmon might be described as rather negative in that I do as little as possible to interfere with a fish as it takes. I certainly never strike. I fish the fly round with the line just resting on the index finger of my upper hand holding the rod. When I feel a fish take, all I have to do is clamp the line, gently raise the rod and tighten into the fish to set the hook. It is as simple as that.

In order to avoid a snatchy take, particularly in fast water where fish can come very quickly at the fly, I fish with a fairly high rod tip. Not vertical, you understand, but with the rod at about 45 degrees. This creates a droop in the line between the tip of the rod and the surface of the water; a fairly short length of slackish line, but just enough to act as a cushion to the fish which takes with a grab.

As the water cools off, and certainly when we are thinking solely in terms of fishing the fly deep and slow, salmon are no longer so quick to turn in the take. There is a method of hooking these fish which is beloved by many ghillies and which I use a lot nowadays. The fly is fished round in the normal way, but this time the line is not touched. It runs free from the reel to the butt ring and beyond. When a fish takes, the reel clicks into action, accelerating as yards of line start to run out. The question is when to tighten. Ghillies are right when they say that, if you wait long enough, the reel will stop turning and that this is the time to set the hook. Certainly there should be no hurry. Often, I have let 4 or 5yd or more of line be drawn off the reel before gripping the line to the rod and tightening into the take.

Not all rivers are of the size of the Spey or Tweed. The Stinchar is a very productive river in south-west Scotland (Arthur Oglesby)

The writer takes a close look at a Loch Lomond fly box, while the late Bill McEwan looks over his shoulder (J. C. Little)

Haaf netters on the River Nith. Is the harvest of wild salmon too heavy? (J. C. Little)

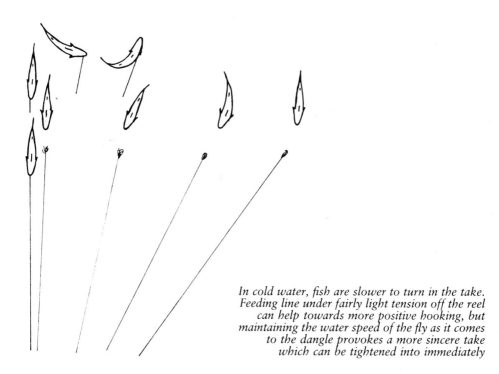

In cold water, fish are slower to turn in the take.
Feeding line under fairly light tension off the reel
can help towards more positive hooking, but
maintaining the water speed of the fly as it comes
to the dangle provokes a more sincere take
which can be tightened into immediately

If nothing else, this method of hooking off the reel has shown me there is no need to throw slack line at a fish, as some fishermen suggest. The reason that this method can work so well is that it positively forces the fisherman to do nothing to interfere with the fish's desire to take the fly.

Incidentally, in order that the fish can take, pull and draw off line from the reel, the ratchet should be set to the minimum, just sufficient to avoid the reel over running and causing a tangle in the line. When the fish is firmly hooked, the drag of the ratchet can be increased cautiously for the time when the fish is being fought.

What I have described so far are the best of the salmon takes, where fish turn in the take. But there is another type, which might be described as the worst of salmon takes.

A couple of seasons ago, fishing through a fine pool on the middle Nith in late autumn, I was wading deep and happily watching my line swim round. I was happy because I was putting out a good length of line, covering the water well but at a shallow angle to ensure that the line came round at minimum speed. I pictured the sinking line carrying down the Brora fly into the depths, the hair wing working in the stream as the fly played at the end of a short leader.

The problem with this long, slow, line technique, combined with deep wading, is that at the point where the fly is hanging directly downstream there is no longer any pressure on the line and so it simply sinks. Just when the fisherman is thinking about making preparations for his next cast, a salmon snatches at the fly. It is suspected that the fish has been tempted by the fly as it fished further out in the stream, but only sufficiently to follow rather than to take. Then, as the fly begins to move upstream, the salmon is convinced and lunges forward. But the fish is in the worst position of all for hooking.

Salmon fishermen have nightmares about fish that take on the dangle. Sometimes all that is felt is a sharp pluck at the line, and then nothing. The salmon has tentatively mouthed the fly, fallen back downstream rather than turning immediately, and the taut line has plucked the hook out of its mouth.

And that was exactly what happened on that late autumn day on the Nith. A short, sharp twitch and then nothing. I swore at the fish, but largely at myself. The solution, I have found, lies not so much in what we do at the actual moment that the fish takes but rather in the few moments before, and this is because the problem stems from a lack of sincerity in the take. It comes down to how we are fishing the fly.

Remember that these tentative takes on the dangle are most prevalent in cold-water conditions. Say we are fishing a long fly as slowly as possible across a stream running at 4mph, and it is sinking in slack water, straight downstream of our position. Because we have fished the fly across as slowly as possible, with a water speed of approximately the same as that of the current, then surely this suggests that we can, and should, maintain that same water speed as the fly enters the slack.

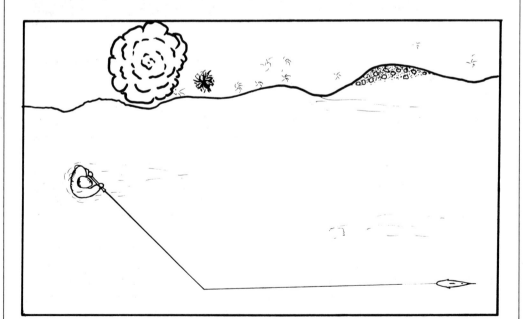

Salmon that take on the dangle, directly downstream of the rod point, are in the worst possible position for hooking

Our primary aim is to hook, play and land salmon with maximum efficiency in minimum time

Most fishermen would agree with this, and it is normal to retrieve a couple of yards of line slowly as the fly comes round to the dangle. This line is retrieved slowly because, in cold-water conditions, we are preoccupied with fishing deep and slow.

However, the fly has just been fishing in the stream with a water speed of 4mph, the equivalent of 6ft per sec and with that in mind, I can confidently retrieve the line and fly in slack water at a far greater pace than is standard practice, and be sure that the long fly is still fishing at a natural speed for a smallish fish trying to escape from a predator.

Since I have been using this minor tactic, accelerating the fly significantly in slack water, takes on the dangle have become far more positive. Some fish will positively engulf the fly, so long as its water speed is maintained at the maximum possible. Of course, where the current is still flowing below the fisherman where the fly is hanging on the dangle, its force must be taken into account. We may halve the rate of retrieve or, if the current was running at close to 4mph it would be illogical to strip the fly back at anything but a very slow pace. Nowadays, for me, hooking fish on the dangle has come down to a matter of inducing a positive take by keeping the fly swimming as it enters slacker water.

I used to have some very clever theories about hooking these fish, once I had induced them to take positively on the dangle. Basically, they involved feeding line to the fish as it took, in order that it could fall back with the current before turning. But in the light of very recent experiences, I have entirely changed my tune.

One fish that I encountered on a northern river a few weeks ago was determined to prove my theories wrong. I was equally determined to prove them right. I was fishing with a high rod, in order to create droop in the line and, as the fly swam round to the dangle in the fading light of dusk, the fly was taken. I had some retrieved line in my hand and allowed the line to draw steadily away through my fingers, taking the slack line and droop with it. I waited, willing the fish to turn but, other than the line gently throbbing, nothing happened. There were no excuses left and so, under the watchful eye of the ghillie, I gently felt for the fish. Up it came, onto the surface, whipping up a lather of foam as it lashed across the surface of the pool. It was obviously nose hooked, behaving in this way, and, inevitably, was not long in shedding the hook; an example of a fish given plenty of droop and line to turn, but to no avail.

What I now find with fish that take on the dangle is that, having concentrated on the water speed of the fly in order to induce a more positive take, the best thing is to tighten into the fish immediately. Indeed, it is practically impossible to do otherwise when one is already actively drawing in line.

I have now described three methods for hooking fish; two which rely on tightening practically as soon as the fish is felt and the other allowing the fish to take line off the reel, under light tension. Some traditionalists will criticise this and, because giving slack line is part of the lore of salmon fishing, totally slack line given at the moment the salmon takes, it is necessary to say a few words on the subject.

Slack line is given to a taking salmon by a fisherman holding a loop of line, possibly as much as 2yd, which he releases when the fish is felt. However, if we picture the exact moment that the salmon takes the fly into its mouth, it is surely obvious that the fly is not entering some infinite vacuum in which it is free to move about. As the fish's mouth closes on the fly, it is practically certain, particularly in the case of a needle-sharp outpoint treble hook, that the point of at least one of the hooks will come in direct contact with some part of its jaw or mouth. The thing to do is to secure that hook-hold immediately. What is the point of feeding slack, other than to place at risk the hook-hold that we have already achieved.

The idea is that feeding slack line will, somehow, cause a belly to form in the line below the fish, thus pulling the fly back toward the scissors of the fish's jaw. Rather than try to argue this point, let me suggest a practical experiment. Get a friend to wade out into the water, holding the end of your line. Then back off from him, some 20yd upstream. Having got the line reasonably taut, as it would

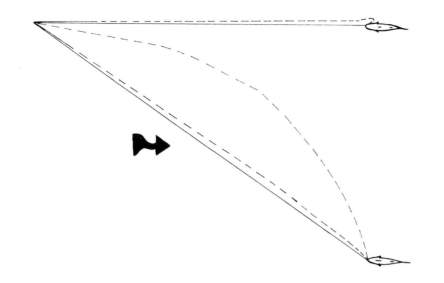

Giving slack line: it takes a long time for slack to have any effect and, unless the fish is directly downstream of the rod tip, how much effect can it have?

be if fishing normally, strip a yard of line off the reel and let it go. After quite a pause, he may mutter that he is not sure but thinks that a wee bit of slack might have arrived at his end. If he is well out in the stream, and you are close into the bank, you can go on to see how many yards of line you need to strip off the reel just to beat the bellying of the line before it curves back into a position that would pull the fly toward the back of the fish's jaw.

Feeding slack line may seem all very well on paper. But, if looked at a little closer, it really doesn't even stand up in theory, let alone in practice. The fisherman feels the fish. It must have the fly in its mouth. He should be setting the hook, not giving the fish every chance to spit it out. If the fisherman can feel the fish, it is a safe bet that the fish can feel the hook.

To my mind, the concept of feeding slack is as outdated as those big, old-fashioned, heavy meat hooks that a previous generation had no alternative but to use for their cold-water fishing. When we think of it, such a hook is the only type that can be taken into a fish's mouth and move about without the point penetrating. They were terrible tools for hooking and, in the old days, it was uncommon to set them firmly in a fish compared to the number that were pulled, pricked and lost. A retired ghillie told me that, in the days of his youth, one of his fishermen, when a salmon took on the dangle, would immediately strip off yards of line and run downstream of the fish before tightening. Even then, more fish were lost than hooked. Today, our largest flies are of the articulated type, armed with a deadly and relatively small treble hook, and our success in hooking and holding fish has increased out of all proportion to the days of our grandfathers.

If you are still not convinced, try this little experiment. Tie a fly, any modern

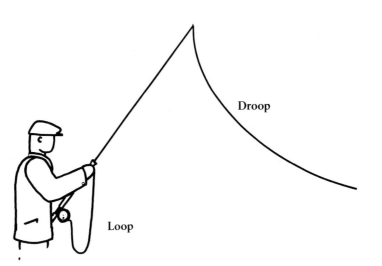

Droop, created by a high held rod, and loop. Droop cushions a snatchy take, but loop seems to have nothing to recommend it

fly incorporating a double or treble hook, to a short length of nylon. Hold the nylon in your right hand, and close your left hand over the hook. Apply pressure by tightening the nylon. You will be very lucky if you can open your hand without one of the hooks sticking in. Now release the tension, open your hand, and the fly simply drops out.

It might be said that by holding the rod tip relatively high, thus creating droop, and by giving those slow-taking, cold-water fish some line off the reel before firmly tightening, we are giving slack. However, we are not, because that line is given under tension. I like giving line off the reel, but faced with the choice between tightening into a fish immediately that it is felt, or feeding slack, I would tighten immediately.

PLAYING FISH

Two things should be done as soon as a fish is hooked. Firstly, check that the line is free to run, that it is not caught round the reel seat or handle or even your wading stick or coat button. Secondly, if you are wading, get out of the water. The sooner that this is done, the better. It is practically impossible to wade out of a strong, boulder-strewn stream and play a fish at the same time without some sort of mishap. People get themselves into all sorts of funny places. On two occasions I have had to go out and literally tow a fellow fisherman, in one case a lady, back to the shore.

The important thing to realise is that a salmon, at this stage in the fight, so long as undue pressure is not applied, may seem indifferent to the fact that it has been hooked. Indeed, some fish will even swim back to their original lie and wait there patiently. But whatever the fish decides to do, put the rod over your shoulder, reel uppermost so that the line can run freely and shuffle your way back to dry land, keeping the rod tip well up.

The position of the rod tip is fundamental to the successful playing of a fish. It should be noted that, when the rod is held vertically, this brings its full cushioning action into effect. If held horizontally, pointing straight at the fish, there is no cushioning between fish and fisherman. Thus, the vertical rod applies minimum strain and maximum cushioning to any fast surges of the salmon. A rod held at about 45 degrees applies heavy strain, but still with a certain degree of cushioning. Maximum pressure is applied by handlining the fish – a fairly desperate manoeuvre, as I feel sure you agree!

For me, the playing of a salmon is still a great thrill. I love the spirit of conflict, and the adrenalin gets fairly pumping; I am not one of those who regard playing a fish as the dullest part of the sport. I cannot imagine a time when I would ever hand over my rod to a ghillie as soon as a fish is hooked and tell him to play it for me. I have known a man who did just that. Having suffered a minor heart attack on the river bank, this was the concession he made to doctor and family not to over-excite himself.

However, some salmon do not put up much of a fight. The first salmon I ever caught, an autumn fish, had obviously travelled far and hard in the time leading up to the moment when it fell for the attractions of my fly. It fought very sluggishly and was soon on the bank. I remember that my thoughts while I played it were little more than 'come on, then' and, when it was finally landed, I really couldn't see what all the fuss was about. I had caught small sea trout that gave me more of a thrill than that 9lb. fish.

The next fish I caught was about one mile upstream from salt water, and fresh off the tide. It fought like fury, one of its long vigorous runs ending in a cartwheeling leap. What excitement; I was desperate to get that fish ashore and breathed a great sigh of relief as a companion netted it for me. It was all that one could ask of a late spring fish: deep, firm and silvery of flank; fresh of flesh and of spirit. Now I knew what all the fuss was about.

As important as the size and strength of the fish is the size and speed of the river. A big, wide river gives a salmon plenty of scope for manoeuvre. Probably due to the side strain we apply, much of the fight is back and forth rather than up and down, so the wider the river the longer the fish is likely to run.

In a strong, powerful stream, where the fish has the full weight of the current behind it, it is no surprise to discover that what was imagined to be an enormous fish is, when seen, of far more modest proportions. Indeed, you don't have to go salmon fishing to experience this. Many of my friends, more used to still-water trout fishing, have admitted thinking that they had hooked a grilse or large sea trout in one of our fast running northern streams only to find that it was a brown trout of barely ¾lb.

But, however much I enjoy playing a fish, do not imagine for one moment that I will prolong the fight in any way. My enjoyment lies in bringing the fight to a conclusion as quickly and efficiently as possible. Watching some folk play a salmon, you soon realise that they are desperately afraid of losing their prize. It is better to take the attitude that if the hook-hold is poor you're likely to lose the fish anyway, so get it over and done with. The only exception to that is with grilse which twist, wriggle and squirm and are masters at shedding hooks. They must be played with a lighter hand and far more care.

It is up to the fisherman to ensure that his tackle is sound and of suitable breaking strain, and that his knots are secure. To lose a fish due to faulty tackle is an admission, not an excuse. It is important to know how much strain your tackle will stand. I have heard it suggested that the novice fisherman should hook his fly into a fence post, although for safety's sake it might be better to remove the fly and simply tie the leader. Then, having run out about 20yd of line, he should pull and pull, putting as much pressure as he dare on the rod, and see if he can break the cast. This was also suggested by Jock Scott in his book *Fine and Far Off* as a method of showing that it was practically impossible to break the lightest of salmon leaders with a straight pull.

Playing a salmon has been described at its simplest as 'when the salmon wants to pull, give him his head; when he stops pulling, then you pull'. And, very largely, that is exactly what happens. The fish plays in a dogged sort of way in the security of deep water. The fisherman lowers his rod to about 40 degrees,

Using a high bank: by getting above a fish, the amount of line in the water, and the risk of the line being drowned, are reduced

piling on the pressure, and draws the fish toward shallower water and the bank. As if suddenly realising his dilemma, the fish then makes a surging rush back toward deep water. As the salmon settles down, pressure is applied again, and the fish drawn back to the point where he has had enough, grows afraid, and tears off back toward deep water once more. So the rod goes up as he runs, giving the fish its head, and then comes down to draw the fish back. At the start of the fight, it may be difficult to control the fish at all, so the rod will be kept pointing skywards to allow the fish to run about and exhaust itself.

Eventually, in the slogging, closing stages of the fight, it will be noted that the fish's energy is beginning to sap. It becomes far easier to draw it toward the shore, and its runs back to deep water become weaker and weaker. Eventually, the fish is too exhausted to continue the fight. It wallows in the shallows, showing its flank, coming to the surface on its side. Now is the time to get it ashore. But I am getting ahead of myself, there are one or two other things that should be mentioned first.

Position and side strain   I know a man who is notorious for standing his ground when a fish is hooked. He chooses his battle station and refuses to budge until the fish is beaten. This may work for him, on the waters that he fishes, but the majority of us would prefer to keep opposite and slightly downstream of the fish. That way, we are able to place maximum strain on the fish, and many a big salmon has been fought to a standstill by a fisherman who got below him and, applying pressure to the full, has slowly towed it downstream, making it fight

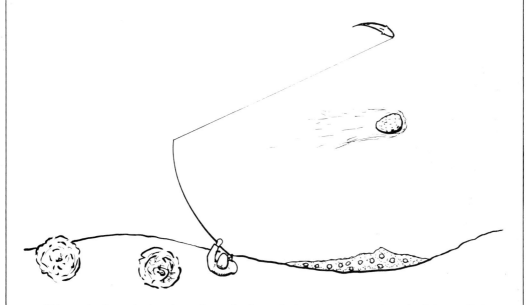

Side strain: by swinging the rod to a horizontal, downstream position, the fish is pulled off balance

Summer salmon can be positive in the take, and Sir William Gordon Cumming is able to demonstrate how to handtail a fish

the full weight of the current, line and rod. Sometimes it can be difficult to keep below a fish. Bill Currie once said to me that they should have a new event at the Game Fair: the 100yd sprint in chest waders! Undoubtedly the course would have to be laid out over shingle, boulders and a heather strewn and steep bank above a deep, raging torrent!

One of the great dangers in playing a salmon, particularly on a wide, strong river such as the Spey or Tweed, is that the line will be drowned. The way to avoid this is to keep the rod tip high in order to keep as much line out of the water as possible. At times, if such a feature is available, it can pay to climb up on a high bank. One fish that I played on the Lochy from a high bank was never able to get more than the leader, and only about half of that, into the water.

On the question of side strain, this kills a fish most efficiently because it throws him off balance. Obviously, by keeping roughly opposite to the fish, and slightly downstream, we are keeping up a steady side strain. However, that strain can be increased by dropping the rod to the horizontal. It should not be pointed at the fish, but rather at right angles to the direction of the line, preferably pointing downstream.

The major risk with lowering the rod to the horizontal is that it brings the line down closer to the water. Indeed, more of the line will be under the surface, and therefore it increases the risk of the line being drowned. Horizontal side strain is not the thing to apply when the fish is far out across a river with a strong central stream. It is a method for finally killing a fish in the closing stages of the fight or where, because the fish is obviously running toward some snag or obstacle, maximum pressure has to be applied.

Length of line and handling   There are many anglers who show great concern when any amount of backing is drawn off the reel. You see them grabbing for the exposed rim. Obviously, you can go too far the other way and allow the fish to run riot. However, there is a happy medium. In terms of playing a fish, give it line and scope, and it will kill itself. In the early stages of the fight, the intention of the tactics employed is not to bully and drag the fish ashore. What we need is for the fish to run and tire itself out. Drawing a fish toward the shore and then letting it run for deeper water, means just that. Draw the fish in until you feel it making that first surge to be away, and then let him go. Point the rod tip up in the air, and give him all the line he wants, within reason. There is little worse than playing a lively salmon on a short line. If the fish will not back off, I would far rather pace backwards to put some distance between us than continue to fight it under the rod tip.

Just as the good driver needs to have a gentle touch on the brakes if he is not to throw his passengers through the windscreen, or throw them forward in their seat belts in more modern parlance, so the fisherman must develop a gentle touch on his brake. So, when we want to increase the pressure, we do this by gently feathering the exposed rim of the reel with our fingers. I emphasise that word 'gentle'. In the heat of the moment it is all too easy to apply far too much pressure and lock the reel. Personally, I have the rod butt tucked into my tummy and continue to hold the rod with both hands, extending the index finger of my right, lower hand to barely touch the rim. Apply pressure carefully, barely tickling the rim and decelerating everything cautiously. Many times you will see a fish ending a long vigorous run with a bout of hectic splashing on the surface. As often as not this is because it has been brought to an abrupt stop by the fisherman applying too much pressure too quickly. The fish cannot go forward or down, and so it comes up. The alternative is a cartwheeling leap. British fish do not leap as freely as North American fish, and when they do there tends to be a reason for it.

What to do when a salmon leaps? If we are honest, we should be able to 'feel' when a fish is about to leap and, by reducing the tension in the line, avoid the risk of the fish crashing down on a taut leader. To be equally honest, how many of us remember to drop our rod tip to a jumping fish? Certainly the theory is

right, in some ways, but how many of us can react in time to make any difference? Note the proviso 'in some ways'. Surely, it is equally correct in theory to say that we should keep the line as taut as possible and, therefore, out of the way of the fish as it lands.

But does it really matter what we say? Look at it this way. I could take a man who had never handled a gun before, and show him how to hit medium high pheasants by teaching him on clay pigeons until the style and movements have become instinctive. But we can't practice dipping our rod tips to leaping salmon on a regular basis, so we just have to do what comes naturally! And, in my case, though I might tell myself off for it in theory, I fail to dip my rod to jumping salmon if they take me by surprise. But if I feel that a fish is about to jump, my instinct is to dip the rod to ease the pressure on it for a moment, in which case I can often persuade it not to come creaming out of the surface. So, no I don't dip my rod to leaping salmon; I dip it to salmon that I think are about to leap. Splitting hairs, it could be said, but there is a definite distinction.

Walking a fish It is possible to walk a salmon like a dog on a lead. The technique is used to lead a salmon away from an obstruction or toward some place that will make things easier when the time comes to get it ashore. Basically, with the fish settled, by clamping the reel spool with the hand and walking steadily along the bank, the fish will follow. This technique can also be employed on the leeward shore of a loch, when a fish is hooked close in and possibly amid a jumble of rocks and boulders. The reel is clamped and the boat rowed out to deep water with the fish obligingly following in its wake.

It is not nearly so easy to tow a fish when the reel handle is turned. The 'click-click-click' of the ratchet seems to be telegraphed down the line to the fish, upsetting it and setting it off on another run. This introduces an incidental aspect of tackle design. The silent salmon reel, where the ratchet is replaced with something more akin to a disc brake, is, from the engineering point of view, a logical alternative. After all, you would hardly fit a ratchet type brake to a car! However, from the point of view of playing a fish, I have found that a fish played off a silent salmon reel is far more likely to sulk, far less likely to indulge in long runs, and the play becomes entirely too prolonged and sluggish.

GRASSING THE FISH

Eventually, the fish is played out and exhausted, and shows this by floating to the surface on its side. Now is the time to get it out of the water.

There are a number of possibilities. Firstly, a gaff could be used. This sharp metal hook, with a gape of a couple of inches, used to be regularly ripped into

Arthur Oglesby with a 40lb Norwegian salmon. In strong, fast rivers, such fish put up an incredible fight

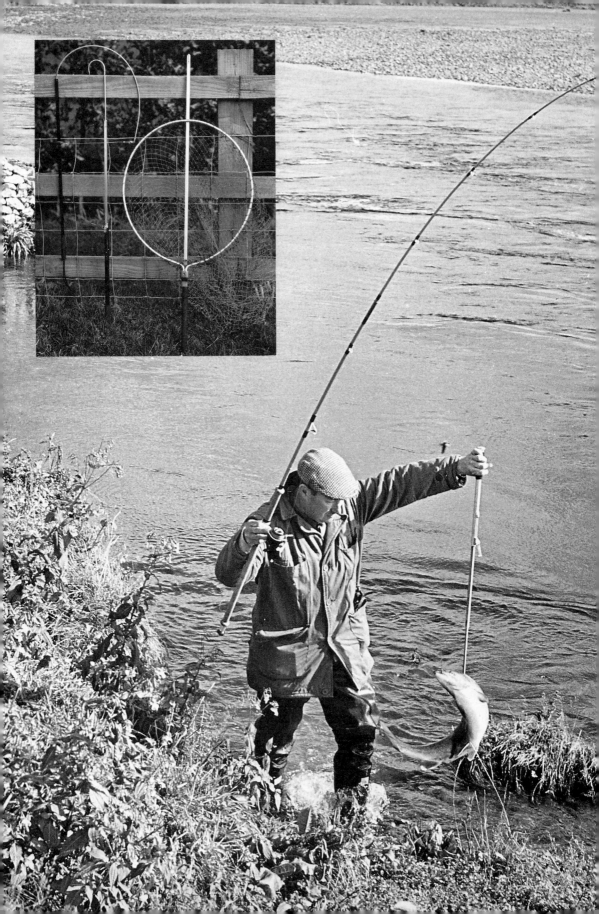

the shoulders of salmon. What a dreadful thing to do to a fish. Gaffs should be avoided whenever possible. Having said that, there are two circumstances where a gaff probably must be used. One is in the case of really big fish such as are encountered in Norway; the other is on some rivers in this country where, due to the nature of the river bank, there is little alternative to a long-handled gaff.

Have you seen the Kirkaig river up in western Sutherland? Peter Hay, the estate factor, has written a small guide book for visiting fishermen and here is part of what he has to say about the Kirkaig Falls pool:

> To gaff a fish one slides down to the right-hand side of the fishing stance, and onto a ledge. There is a rope attached to the rock as a hand-hold. When gaffed, the gaff and fish are handed up to the angler who must take care not to let the fish off the gaff and drop on the head of his ghillie!

I would only add that waders are not advised for the Upper Beat, but climbing boots very definitely are.

Then there are mechanical tailers in the form of a sort of snare at the end of a handle. These were very popular some years ago, but have fallen out of favour. They are fiddly brutes at the best of times. God gifted us with the best mechanical tailers of all, our hands, so why carry around extra ironmongery?

Nets have replaced tailers in popularity. There was a time when it was thought that you needed a ghillie or companion to wield the net and, in the days when salmon nets were produced in the local smithy, this was undoubtedly true. Today, we have lightweight but strong alloy-framed nets which can be easily worked single-handed.

Of all the types of salmon nets, the Gye with its rigid, circular head sliding on a rectangular handle, is far and away the most popular. Having listened to Bill Currie tirelessly singing the praises of his net which, he says, he would not be seen salmon fishing without, I got a Gye type. I do not use it all the time, but it has plucked more than a few salmon from awkward places, and it certainly always travels with me when I go fishing even if it does not always get an airing, or a wetting. The main point about netting a salmon, whether for yourself or another angler, is to get the net into the water and draw the fish over it. There is nothing worse than to play out a fish only to find that the chap who has volunteered to net it is chasing it all over the place. There is no alternative, no time for good manners; tell him to get the hell out of it.

Netting, to my mind, is the method to use where deep water flows close in to the bank. When I see a fisherman or his ghillie netting a salmon on a gently shelving, pebbly beach, I cannot help wondering who is trying to justify what.

It is a simple matter to beach an exhausted salmon, so long as the terrain is suitable. At best, it will be done onto a long bank of gently shelving gravel, but it

Time was when few salmon fishermen would be seen without a gaff. Today, they are only used in exceptional circumstances; (inset) Mechanical means of grassing a fish: tailer, gaff and net

Shirley Deterding using a Gye net for husband Jimmy. Note the hold, close to the ring of the net, to ease the strain on the handle when the salmon is lifted from the water

can just as easily be done in a tiny bay, so long as the gradient is none too steep. I prefer to wade out a little way from the bank and lead the fish in ahead of me. Then, as its head and flank emerge from the water and onto the beach, it is a simple matter to reach down and grasp it by the wrist of the tail, and carry it back from the river bank.

Hand tailing is very much the same process except that, instead of leading the fish inshore, the rod is pointed upstream and the fish, on a short line, is allowed to drift downstream alongside the angler who reaches down, grips the fish by its wrist, just above the tail, and lifts the fish from the water and onto the bank. It sounds very simple and indeed it is, but it is as well to get in some practice on dead fish before trying it on a live one. I still go cold at the memory of a man, who I presumed to be experienced in these matters, hand tailing a fish for me and promptly dropping it. The hooks came out, and that was the fastest that I have ever covered five yards; I went down on the salmon like a full-back falling on a loose ball in front of his posts! Hand tailing takes coolness and deliberation, something that comes with experience. I, for one, will be pleased if people stick to practising on their own fish.

One further method of beaching a salmon might be mentioned. I have only seen it in action on the Lochy. As I drew a salmon up onto a beach, a local angler strode into the water and applied the 'welly boot' technique, kicking the fish high into the air and up on the bank. I was too dumbfounded to say a word.

As a last point, always carry a 'priest' with which to 'administer the last rites'. My own is a length of alkathene pipe with a piece of solid brass inserted at one end. A couple of taps on the back of the fish's head put an end to any suffering that it might be experiencing. I do not know, but I imagine that taking a fish from water into air may be rather like holding a man's head under water. We are sportsmen, and our quarry deserves respect. Do not leave it flapping feebly on the bank while you go off in search of a suitable rock or stick.

9

SPORT ON THE LOCH

I picture my first Hebridean salmon as if the proud capture was made only yesterday. I was not yet in my teens, and many seasons have passed since then, but that hard fighting and wild spirit still haunts my mind. It flashes back through crystal clear waters, jigging and reeling to rid itself of the tiny Wickham's Fancy embedded in its jaw. That first salmon came to my fly when I journeyed with my father to fish the Hebridean lochs so temptingly described by Negley Farson in his wonderful book *Going Fishing*. Farson captivated the imaginations of the wartime generation of fishermen. In his footsteps, my father and I learnt the pleasures of drifting the lonely lochs for salmon and sea trout.

In the years that followed, my father and I made an annual pilgrimage to the Atlantic seaboard. We fished in Ireland, the Hebrides and the West Highlands. Summer holidays spelt lochs, salmon, grilse and sea trout. They combined the father and son's shared joys in boats and fishing. And, a very important point, the lochs provided sport with salmon in high summer, a time when the more noted rivers of the mainland were suffering from low water and high temperatures. This provision of sport in the troublesome days of summer is as true now as it was then. A few years ago, when I forsook my career in estate management, we lived for a time in the West Highlands, on the border between Argyll and Inverness. I seized the opportunity to fish many of the region's famous and some of its lesser known waters. Even now, when we have returned to the Scottish Borders, many of the lochs are within a short driving distance. So, you are not to imagine that all I relate is hidden in the mists of time! As soon as the warm weather comes each year, and the lawns cry out to be cut, I am packing my bags and heading north-west.

It is so very hard to describe the lochs. There is that eternal, soft western sky. Like the inhabitants of their shores, the lochs have a quiet charm and character of their very own. But when the wind tears through the glen, skimming white-topped rollers down the loch to crash on the rocky leeward shores, their anger is awesome. Rough conditions can offer superb fishing. On a recent trip to Mull, our ghillie described the eccentric behaviour of a turn-of-the-century, retired military man. He would only venture out in the very wildest of weather. His answer to the lashing rain and spumes of spray was to strip completely naked. He would perch in the stern of the boat, wielding a mighty greenheart rod while two cowering and prayer muttering ghillies manned the oars and fought to keep

Gerald Panchaud plays a Harris salmon in the sea. Hebridean fishing has a charm of its own, and the fish write their own rules

the boat's bow into the wind. The old man roared out his defiance to the elements and the fish in a way made possible only by a lifetime spent within earshot of the barrack square and stable yard.

I know it may sound corny, but I cannot fail to mention the solitude, the smell of peat and myrtle, the earth steaming after summer rains, and swollen burns cascading from the mist-shrouded peaks to feed the hungry loch. I breathe in the sights, scents and sounds; the haunting cries of moor fowl, oyster catcher and curlew; quiet Gaelic voices; wild fish and wilder sport. It all creates an attitude of mind, a type of freedom. Nothing is guaranteed and all plans are for breaking. All plans, that is, but the one to return to the ageless scene described by a host of writers who came, saw and left their souls forever in the twilight land.

Loch fishing does not appeal to everybody, and thank goodness for that. Half of the attraction, for me, lies in the solitude. On many of the smaller lochs of the

West Highlands and Hebrides, one boat is sufficient and two would be overcrowding, and I would not fish such a water where the management did not agree with that feeling. The bigger lochs, such as Maree, Shiel and Lomond, can carry an astounding number of boats and still allow their occupants to 'get away from it all'. I have fished Lomond on a holiday weekend when there might have been fifty boats out and still felt that, other than those in the boat with me, I had only the buzzards soaring lazily above the islands for company. Those who have only experienced that dreadful, nose to tailing road on the western shore and the caravan sites and tartan doll shops, cannot begin to imagine the tranquillity of the 'bonnie banks' of the east and the islands.

Those of you who seek summer sport with salmon and enjoy boats, those who would rather stand on deck during a rough ferry crossing, all those who will pause to watch the soaring eagle or timid roe buck as he drinks his fill on the evening shore, will recognise the lure of the loch. And when you have tasted it, you will always return for more.

LOCH FLIES

Bob flies   I associate loch fishing with a brisk breeze and a running wave. Clouds scurry from the south-west, bringing soft showers and sunny spells. The drizzle dries away and a lazy sun blinks from behind the clouds. As the flies are worked steadily back through the wave, right up to the gunwale of the boat, there is a sudden dashing rise and a glimpse of deep, silvery flank. The first fish of the day is on.

It is normal to fish with two flies on the loch cast for salmon, a small fly on the point or tail of the cast and a rather larger fly, probably with a palmered hackle run from throat to tail, fished on a dropper. We refer to the latter as a 'bob' fly which aptly describes the way that it should be fished – cutting up through the waves and bobbing onto and into the surface. Sea trout, in particular, love a bob fly fished skittering through the surface of the loch. At times they go crazy for it. It is a satisfying way of taking these fish and very deadly. Salmon will also rise to a bob fly as it dances and trips along the water although, it has to be said, without the gay abandon of their smaller cousins. Nevertheless, the bob fly is fundamental in our approach to catching either species, so we should spend some time considering its attractions.

I do not hold to the point of view that the bob fly, in regard to salmon and sea trout, represents an insect of any sort. I acknowledge that it could do so, but feel that this is of only minor importance. I am convinced that we are really representing the panic stricken flight of small prey fish as they scutter along the surface in a desperate attempt to escape the jaws of predatory fish that come charging in to attack from beneath. If you are familiar with coastal waters, you will have seen gatherings of gulls as they wheel and dive into a sea set boiling by thousands of little fish. The birds repeatedly plummet into the water, surfacing each time with a sliver of silver in their bills. Why do the little fish not swim deeper? It is because larger, predatory fish are hammering up into their shoals from beneath, holding the prey fish 'between the devil and the deep blue sea'.

The response of a sea trout to a stimulus that mimics the behaviour of prey fish on the surface is far greater than that of the salmon. The mimicry is more reminiscent of the former's coastal and estuary feeding than the deep-sea adventures of the latter. The sea trout responds with gusto, but the salmon is not so convinced. He takes his time and carefully inspects the goods before committing himself. Often he will detect the deceit and turn warily away. But the bob fly has caught his interest, even if he does not take.

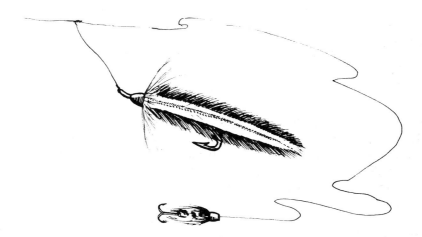

A large elver fly on the bob and a tiny tube on the point can be very productive on some Hebridean lochs

Two distinct schools of thought have emerged in regard to the salmon's cautious approach to the bob fly. The first sees the bob fly as little more than a piscatorial dinner gong to attract the fishes' attention to the far smaller fly fishing on the tail of the cast. This type of 'little and large' combination is wildly productive on Grimersta on the Isle of Lewis where many feel that the pattern of bob fly is unimportant just so long as the fly is big, size 4 or even 2. The Muddler Minnow with its exaggerated head of clipped deer hair for maximum disturbance is very popular, as is Arthur Ransome's Elver Fly with wings of vulturine guinea-fowl feathers extending as much as 2in behind the eye of the hook. An occasional fish will actually take these big flies, but they are really regarded simply as attractors to excite the interest of a salmon which will then take the tail fly – a tiny double-hooked fly, size 10 to 12, or a wisp of a tube fly armed with a minute treble.

Grimersta's reputation for producing salmon has few rivals. It may seem natural, therefore, that 'if it's good enough for Grimersta, it's good enough for . . .' is the right attitude but this is not always so. On many waters that I have fished, it is found that a relatively small and quite lightly dressed bob fly will not only serve as an attractor to salmon, but will catch them as well. Now, I have to say immediately that I have never fished Grimersta, and must bow to the experience and knowledge of its aficionados, but it does strike me as odd that a fly which raises and hooks a salmon on the big, mainland salmon lochs should not be capable of achieving the same on the relatively shallow waters of Grimersta. But there we are; there is little so strange as salmon fishing and salmon. I know that only a fool would journey to Grimersta without some big flies for the bob position, but it would be interesting to experiment.

Fly pattern and size Hair-winged flies are popular on many salmon lochs, particularly those of the Hebrides, but when I first fished on Lomond with the late Bill McEwan he was quick to tell me that he had never enjoyed any success with them there. If any wing could be described as typical of a Lomond fly it would probably be the white-tipped turkey found on such flies as the Ian Wood, Turkey and Mixed among others. Why it is that a wing of grey-squirrel tail is not similarly effective, with its white tip over grey brown? I cannot explain any more than why the big bob fly is a favourite on Grimersta. Some things we can explain, others we simply have to accept unless we can prove otherwise.

In compiling my own short list of favoured flies for use on the salmon loch, I find that I tend toward patterns with a hen pheasant or bronze mallard wing, a tinsel or lurex body, and a lightly palmered hackle. Examples that immediately spring to mind are the Silver or Gold Invicta, possibly a Dunkeld and certainly a Dark Mackerel. Bulk is a most important consideration. We could fish with roughly tied, seal-fur bodied and heavily hackled flies for salmon, but we should have to reduce the size. Often, that is exactly what we do. For example, if I was swopping one of the tinsel bodied Invictas for a standard Invicta with its yellow fur body, or a Mallard and Yellow which can be very productive, I would probably drop the size from, say, an 8 to a 10.

A Gold Invicta, tied on a size 10 of 12 double hook, is a great favourite of mine for the tail of the cast. The palmered ginger hackle filters the gold tinsel of the body, creating glint rather than glitter. This combination, with a light touch of dyed blue guinea-fowl at the throat, with a sparse wing of hen pheasant tail fibres, has sobriety of hue. It is a marvellous fly.

Silver Invicta: any fly that combines a tinsel body with a palmered hackle and feather wing from a hen pheasant or mallard, is a good fly to have on the loch cast

Salmon in a boat. Favourite patterns and sizes of loch flies vary with location and conditions

The feather wing, tinsel body, palmered hackle patterns have served me well in the past and therefore I have great confidence in them and fish them most of the time. However, they are not the only flies that I use on the lochs. If I was fishing a Hebridean water, I would certainly be keen to try a small, hair-winged double on the tail – a Hairy Mary, Garry Dog or a Thunder Stoat. Equally, a small Butcher, fished on the bob in a light wave on a bright day, has taken fish for me.

To be more specific as to size of fly, if you are ever lucky enough to fish Grimersta you will almost certainly start the day with a size 2 or 4 on the bob and probably a tiny tube fly, the body being little more than ¼in, on the point. On other waters, with which the vast majority of us are concerned, we may choose the same tiny fly for the point, but our bob fly will be much smaller. It depends very largely upon the height of the wave. In a real swash-buckler, I would make a start with a size 6, possibly an 8, on the bob. My tail fly would be a size 10 double. In average conditions, I would stick with the 8 on the bob, but reduce the tail fly to a size 12 or minute tube fly, giving the hooking potential associated with tiny treble hooks. In the lightest of breezes, I would feel that I had already gone small enough in the tail fly, and choose size 12 for both positions on the cast.

TACKLE

Leaders and lines   First in line between the flies and the fisherman is the leader, or cast as I still refer to it when it bears more than one fly. Call it what you will, I normally fish with a cast of about 11ft, a foot shorter than my rod. I make it up with a dropper to take the bob fly set about 4ft from the junction with the main line. I like the dropper to be 3in to 4in long. I seldom fish lighter than 8lb, would normally choose 10lb, and will happily use 12lb in a good wave.

I could hardly describe my casts as tapered, but I would normally choose to employ 12lb nylon between the main line and the bob fly as heavier nylon is apt to stand out from the cast rather than wrap round it, then a 4ft length of 10lb blood knotted to the final 3ft length of 8lb leading to the tail fly. As to the main casting line, I have lost count of the times that I have seen a green or brown line outfishing a white one. Equally, I seldom fish with a floating line on the loch for salmon. From those two statements, you will make your own judgement on my opinion of white, floating lines for this type of work!

The floating line is a marvellous tool for the fast fishing of big and hairy sea trout flies. Being light, it is caught in the breeze and acts like a spinnaker sail, lifting the cast and dragging the bob fly. In sea trout fishing, we take this further by handlining our flies quickly. Fish a fast fly for sea trout and they will attack it with gusto, mucho gusto. However, a salmon will usually ignore a fly fished at very high speeds and requires a far steadier approach. An intermediate at best, or a slow sinker, settles everything down. It is not caught so easily by the wind.

At the other end of the scale, when we are faced with a whisper of breeze and the lightest ripple, our tactics will be to fish fine and far off with a steady retrieve and probably an extra-long leader. A floating line, in such conditions, will create a wake on the surface. Far better to have our line a few inches below the surface rather than dragging across the top of the water. Again, the case is proven for a slow sinking line.

Rods and reels   If you intend to spend some time fishing the salmon lochs, I would advise you to invest in as long a rod as you can handle comfortably. Carbon fibre allows us to fish a longer rod, far longer than any other material. I prefer to fish with a single-handed rod on the loch, so my own choice falls on a length of 12ft. This rod, incidentally my own is a Grey's of Alnwick Kielder, gives me great line control and keeps the bob fly on the surface for a large proportion of the retrieve. Rated AFTM 5–7 it is a long, supple rod, a marvellous buffer against the short but hectic fight of grilse and sea trout on both loch and river.

Those whose wrists are not kept in regular practice may find such a length of rod to be quite tiring at the end of a long day due to the increased leverage, particularly when casting a long line in light conditions. They may prefer a somewhat shorter rod. However, I could not advise a shorter rod than 10½ft in order to be fishing at anything like full potential in all conditions.

Finally, there is the reel, which should have a large but fairly narrow drum in order to hold plenty of line and backing. It should be uncomplicated, totally devoid of gimmickry, and reliable in use. In recent years I have relied heavily on reels marketed by Leeda Tackle for use with single-handed salmon and sea trout rods. I have nothing but praise for the Leeda Dragonfly reels. Their lightweight carbon construction is specifically designed for use with the modern generation of carbon rods. The Kingsize 100 and Imperial 120, both with exposed rim and variable check, offer all one could look for. I also have a Leeda Magnum which, being made of metal, is far heavier than the Dragonfly and is therefore particularly suited to those who prefer a heavy reel to balance the leverage inherent in long rods.

FISHING THE LOCH

The fisherman who knows his rivers but is new to the loch may be daunted at the prospect of a sheet of seemingly featureless water. The obvious course of action is to hire a local ghillie or boatman. A good one will be intimate with the hidden secrets of the bays and promontories, constantly adjusting the line of the drift with a gentle stroke on the oars. There will be few resting places for salmon in his loch that he does not know to the nearest yard, and he should be able to stalk the fish, easing the boat to windward as the fisherman searches the likely water with his duet of flies.

However, there may not be a local guide and then the fisherman is left to make do as best he can. He may miss out on some of the less obvious spots but there are some fairly clear signs to look for as pointers to salmon lies and, if the fisherman concentrates on these, he has every chance of success.

Where to fish As a general rule, the salmon prefers water of less than 10ft, whereas the majority of sea trout prefer deep-water lies in the 10–20ft range. Over the seasons, I have learnt to concentrate my efforts for salmon in water of 3–7ft. Obviously then, on the majority of salmon lochs we will be looking to the shorelines although, on smaller and shallower lochs, this range may cover the entire area.

The shore itself can tell us a great deal. As with the river, a steep rock face dropping straight down into the water is an obvious sign that it is likely to be too deep to hold fish. A gently shelving shore, on the other hand, will maintain the same gradient for some distance out into the loch, underwater, and will probably offer a relatively large area within our favoured range of depths. Another point to look for is a tumble of rocks and boulders on the shoreline. Again, these are likely to extend out underwater, and salmon love to lie with their belly on a slab of rock.

On a day of flat calm we gave up the fly rods, put out two trolls and motored gently along, parallel to the shore. As we passed a rocky groyne extending into the loch, we knew we were passing over a likely place. As we travelled on, the long lines trailing away in our wake, my companion started a countdown from fifty, '. . . six, five, four'. He never got to three. He was too busy with the wildly bucking rod as twelve pounds of silver leapt far behind. Later in the day, at a similar spot, the countdown went to zero, there was a slight pause, and there was another fish. Rocky promontories from gently shelving shores; what fantastic sport they can produce.

Equally, we must never forget that salmon have returned in order to spawn and will complete their mating rituals in the tiny burns running into the lochs. That is one reason why the mouth of a burn is a good place to try and this is one spot where a salmon may be caught from the shoreline, as many an après-lunch cast will testify. The inflow and outflow of rivers are other good spots always worth reconnaissance. The inflows of burns and rivers, beside being of importance in regard to spawning fish waiting for suitable conditions to run up them, may also carry sediment and debris into the loch, creating shallow areas.

Two in a boat Having decided where to fish, the only matter to be settled is whether two fishermen can operate from the same boat, or if it is to be a solo effort. As a general rule, many of the smaller lochs of the West of Ireland and Hebrides yield their best to one man fishing with a ghillie. In saying ghillie, I include those times when two fishermen take it in turns to man the oars.

On larger waters – lochs such as Maree, Assynt, Hope, Eilt, Sheil and so on – where some drifts may be measured in miles rather than yards, as on Lomond's Endrick Bank, there is normally plenty of scope for two rods. In fact, it is not uncommon to see a fly rod at either end of the boat and a dapping pole jutting up in the centre. However, even on these larger lochs, there are times and places where it might be better to operate with only one rod. I shall consider this further in the section on cross-wind fishing.

Downwind fishing The simplest method of presenting the flies is to cast straight downwind from a free drifting boat. The boat is moving sideways and the flies are continually covering new water as they are slowly drawn back, prior to the next cast. This is classic wet-fly fishing on the loch. It is an ideal technique for fishing a long shoreline when the wind is blowing parallel to it.

In order to give the flies the appearance of life, they must be retrieved faster than the speed of the drifting boat. The faster the drift, the faster the retrieve must be made. For example, if the boat is drifting downwind before a spanking fine breeze at 4mph, the flies must be retrieved upwind at 6mph in order to give them an apparent speed of 2mph. At a more moderate drift of 2mph, the flies would need to be retrieved at 4mph to maintain the same apparent speed. The latter might be too great for a salmon; an apparent speed of only 1mph might be closer to our requirement.

The flies can be retrieved in a number of ways. Some fishermen favour the figure-of-eight retrieve but, while it may be suitable for a light breeze, I regard it as far too fiddly a task to keep up for a full day on the loch. To tell the truth, it has all the appeal of darning socks or crochet. I like to get on with the job in hand. As I cast the line, I hook it over the index finger of my right hand, which holds the rod. I reach up with my left hand, taking hold of the line just below the right hand and then draw the line back to the full extent of my arm, the speed of the draw being dependent on the rate of drift, as already described. I then let go of the line with my left hand, gripping it again with the index finger of my right, over which it has been running during the draw, and raise my rod slightly during the time that the left hand is reaching forward to start another draw on the line. The slight raising of the rod is an important point; I like the retrieve to be fluid and continuous.

After one or two more draws have been made on the line, I raise the point of the rod at the same time as making one final draw, causing the bob fly to scutter along the surface – a killing moment. As the rod comes right back beyond the vertical, drawing the flies right under the gunwale of the boat, I make a roll cast. This is the easiest and safest way to cast in a downwind drift. How I hate to fish with a man who insists on an overhead cast over his inboard shoulder, and it is sheer purgatory for the ghillie. I aim the roll cast high, the wind helping to carry out the retrieved line through the rod rings, and settle the line down lightly like the proverbial thistledown.

The length of line fished is very largely dependent on the strength of the wind and thus the height of the waves. In light breezes, as I have said before, it is necessary to fish fine and far off, and I like to work with 20yd of line or thereabouts. With a good wave to hide our antics and the coarseness of our tackle, however, we can shorten the length of line to as little as three rod lengths, fishing in the classic short-line technique perfected on the Irish loughs where they seem to stroke the waters, using a short line, with very little retrieve other than the raising of the rod.

The downwind technique has caught many thousands of fish in the past and will continue to do so in the future. It is certainly the most practised technique on the larger lochs. However, other than small attempts to fish the fly slightly outside the path of the boat, it confines the fishing to a narrow strip of water, and there are other ways to fish a fly. To a large extent, if not totally, the following method depends on the presence of a skilled boatman, be he amateur or professional. Make no mistake, on many lochs a good man on the oars is worth his weight in fish.

Fishing across the wind We talk of a 'drift' on the loch as defining the strip of water over which the boat travels. However, in some cases the boat will not simply be allowed to drift at the dictates of the wind, and the oars will have to be manned. The classic example is a leeward shore. In a strong breeze, with waves breaking over the shoreline rocks, the leeward, downwind shore can offer tremendous sport. It has to be approached in the correct manner, however, with the boat held off and manoeuvred in a zigzag fashion.

Helene Panchaud with a fine catch from Loch Voishimid, Isle of Harris

An oarsman who acts in sympathy with his fisherman can materially improve the presentation of the flies, and close teamwork can yield extra fish. The fisherman casts and, as his flies alight on the water, the oarsman makes his first stroke, driving the boat away from the shore and pulling the flies along. As the boat loses way, the fisherman starts his retrieve, accelerating as the boat begins to drift back inshore and raising his rod to bring the bob fly tripping along the surface. Slowly and carefully, the team edge their way across the shoreline.

I am lucky in that the majority of anglers and ghillies that I have fished with have been good oarsmen. Some of them have rowed as a sport in its own right, as I did in the past. There is a craft to rowing, feathering the oars to minimise disturbance; a long and steady pull rather than two short splashy ones and an almost delicate turn of the bows; a light touch that only comes with experience. An indifferent oarsman, even if claiming the right to be considered as better than nothing, may disturb fish that could otherwise have been caught. If you are lucky enough to obtain the services of an expert ghillie, watch and learn.

I am always ready to take my turn on the oars on a leeward shore. People differ, but I take a quiet satisfaction in handling a boat well. The gentle manoeuvring required to fish my companion's flies right into the shore, possibly having to pick a course through a maze of jagged rocks and boulders in rough water, makes the hooking of a fish and leading it out to be fought in deep water, very much a shared pleasure.

This technique can also be used to fish a downwind drift, simply by zigzagging the course of the boat. There is a deadly fascination for salmon in a fly that is drawn across the waves rather than directly into them. It is possible to fish the fly in this cross-wave style on a straight downwind drift by casting out to the side of the boat and drawing the rod back across your front, but it is no real substitute for the services of a competent oarsman, gently working the boat back and forth across the wind.

Hooking and playing I can offer very little advice on hooking a salmon that comes to the fly fished on the tail of the cast. There may be a slight swirl on the surface but, more often, the first thing you know is that there is a salmon on the end of the line. The tiny double hook, or treble if you are fishing a tube fly, has already done its work and there is nothing more that you can do, other than maintain a firm pressure.

It is the salmon's rise to the bob fly that creates the greatest anxiety. Suddenly, there is a whorl on the surface and you glimpse a silvery flank, maybe even the head of the fish and its open mouth. The temptation is to strike hard, but you must do absolutely nothing. Treat this rise as you would a big and lazy trout on the chalk streams. You must give the salmon time to turn down with the fly. Strike, and you will simply pull the fly out of its mouth.

When the fish disappears, gently feel for it by raising the rod tip. When you make contact, set the hook with a purposeful, but not too hard, flick of the wrist. Forget all about striking. You do not strike at a salmon; you feel for it, then tighten into it, setting the hook.

Some say the most difficult of all fish to hook is the one that takes the fly in the very last moment of the retrieve when the rod tip is way back over the shoulder, and the hands pulled well apart. The best solution I can offer is to clamp the line to the rod with the index finger of the right hand, and flick out the line as if you were performing your normal roll cast. Even then there will be a brief but seemingly never ending moment as you hurry to draw in line and discover whether a strong contact has really been made. Just one more of the joys of fishing for salmon!

INDEX

ACKNOWLEDGEMENTS

First and foremost, I must acknowledge the help and encouragement of my mother and father. Few children have the opportunities given to them to fish from such an early age. No doubt I would have become a salmon fisherman eventually, but this book would have been a lot later in the writing. For that, and a host of memories of days and weeks spent by river and loch, I thank you from the bottom of my heart.

Many famous figures in the world of salmon fishing have given freely of their time and advice. It started on the Spey with Captain Tommy Edwards and Jack Martin. Many of the leading writers whose words I studied so avidly in my teenage years and twenties were later to become acquaintances, and some of them friends and fishing companions. John Ashley Cooper gave me great encouragement when I first ventured into the world of sporting magazines and writing. Bill Currie had an enormous effect on my formative fishing years, so it was a real pleasure to fish and learn alongside him. Fishing the drifts of Loch Lomond will never be the same without the quiet wit and charm of Bill McEwan; a fine man without the slightest trace of dogma. Arthur Oglesby, a true gentleman, kind and considerate, and a great fisherman. Then there is Hugh Falkus with his boundless enthusiasm and original thinking on the sport. To all these, and a host of fishing friends who, as they say, are too numerous to mention, but no less in my thoughts, my gratitude.

I must mention Arthur Oglesby once more. Together with Eric Chalker, the two of them have provided nearly all the fine photographs for this book. I thank you both.